To Amy

Keep enjoying life
Amy
Thank You For Your
Support!

Apostle Rhetta Jackson-Fair

Thy Kingdom Come

Thy Kingdom Come

Apostle Rhetta Jackson-Fair

Thy Kingdom Come
Copyright © 2024 Apostle Rhetta Jackson-Fair

All rights reserved. No part of this publication may be reproduced, distributed, or transmitted in any form or by any means, including photocopying, recording, or other electronic or mechanical methods, without the prior written permission of the publisher, except in the case of brief quotations embodied in critical reviews and certain other noncommercial uses permitted by copyright law.

First Edition: April 2024

ISBN: 979-8-218-41089-6 (Paperback)
ISBN: 979-8-218-41090-2 (Hardcover)
ISBN: 979-8-218-41091-9 (eBook)

Rhetta Jackson
943 Alden Dr.
Toms River, NJ, 08753

https://apostlerhetta.com/

Table of Contents

Preface i

Chapter 1 1
    Introduction to Kingdom Building 1
    Understanding Kingdom Citizenship and Kingdom Building 3
    Why is Jesus King of Kings and Lord of Lords? 5
    What is The Kingdom of God? 7
    How and Why Are True Christians Adopted into The Family of God? 10
    What is our God-Given Purpose as Kingdom Citizens? 13
    How Do We Accomplish Our Purpose? 15
    Thy Kingdom Come 18

Chapter 2 22
    The Power of Commonalities 22
    We Must Be Deliberate and Intentional About Our Kingdom Associations 25
    Intentionally Search for Those That Are Like-minded 27
    Listen to the Ideas of Others 30
    Be Open to Sharing Your Ideas with Others as God Leads 33
    Embrace Those Outside Your Immediate Circle 36
    Become Willing to Partner with Other Kingdom Builders Who Share the Same Commonalities 39
    We Have More in Common Than We Differ 41

Chapter 3 47
    Breaking Down Barriers 47
    Kingdom Citizens Break Down Societal Barriers by Living & Enforcing Kingdom Principles 49
    Stand Firm on Kingdom Principles 51
    Understand that Warfare is Part of Breaking Down Barriers 54
    Be Strategic 57
    Remain Faithful to God and Your Team 59
    Remember The Goal 62

God Has Given Us Power & Authority to Break Down Barriers That Would Hinder The Kingdom of God 65

Chapter 4 71

Embracing Diversity 71

Diversity is the Spice of Life 73

Visit Local Community Groups 75

Be Open to Fellowship with Others In and Outside Your Religion 77

Join a Prayer Group 80

Fellowship with Different Cultures 82

Travel and Visit Other Countries 85

United We Stand, Divided We Fall 87

Chapter 5 92

The Role of Empathy 92

We Must See Others Through God's Perspective 94

Get to Know and Understand the Strengths and Weaknesses of Those You Partner With 97

Share Your Strengths and Weaknesses 99

Commit to Uplifting Others 101

Allow Others to Uplift You 104

Embrace Other People's Perspectives 106

In a Healthy Relationship, There Should Never Be Any Partiality 108

Chapter 6 113

Financial Unity 113

Be Willing to Sow and Invest into The Kingdom Financially 115

We Have Greater Success with Good Partners 117

Be Honest with Those You Partner with About Your Portion of the Financial Contribution 120

Come Together and Seek Out and Sow into Good Soil/Kingdom Soil 122

Keep the Goal Before You 124

Pray for a Great Harvest 126

It Takes Two to Build and Two Is Better Than One 127

Chapter 7 130
God's Purpose in Relationships 130
You Will Go Through Spiritual Warfare When Kingdom Building 132
Make Time to Meditate on The Word of God with Your Partner 134
There is Power in Prayer When Two or More Like-Minded People Come Together 136
When One Partner Deals with Adversity, the Other Partner Can Fill In .. 138
Always Be Willing to Encourage and Uplift 140
Be Quick to Forgive One Another 143
One Can Chase a Thousand Evil Spirits Away but Two Spirit Filled People Can Put 10,000 Demons to Flight 145

Chapter 8 149
Navigating Challenges Together 149
True Partnership is Not 50/50 151
Admit Your Shortcomings 153
Be Quick to Hear 155
Be Slow to Anger 157
Be Willing to Step in and Do More Than Your Share 159
Remember There's Always Someone Smarter Than You 161
True Partnership is Becoming Acquainted and Maturing Together 163

Chapter 9 167
Leadership in Kingdom Building 167
Good Leaders are Never Afraid to Raise Up Other Leaders 168
Don't Take on Everything If Others Are Willing to Help You 170
Identify Gifts in Others & Distribute the Workload Equally 172
Keep the Vision Before You 173
Don't Mimic What Others Are Doing; Be Strategic 175
Live & Encourage a Balanced Lifestyle 176
Good Leaders Do Not Compete; They Collaborate 178

Chapter 10 182
Community Outreach and Impact 182

In Order to Have a Successful Community Outreach, You Must Find the Needs of Your Community 184

Speak to Your Neighbors 186

Communicate with Successful Community Outreaches to Form Relationships and Collaborations.. 188

Look into Your Local Salvation Army 191

Boys and Girls Club 192

YMCA... 194

In The Kingdom, There Are No Big "I's" and Little "You's". We Are All in This Together. 196

Chapter 11 199

Educational Empowerment... 199

Never Stop Learning 200

Enforce Ongoing Education.. 201

Be Aware of What's Going on in Current Events in Society 204

Learn About Politics 205

Study Different Languages 207

Learn and Embrace Different Cultures as Long as It Does Not Go Against Your Spiritual Values 208

Knowledge is Power! 210

Chapter 12 213

Legacy of Love 213

The Most Important Part of The Kingdom Builder's Life is the Lives We Change and the Legacy We Leave Behind 214

Begin Raising Up a Successor 216

Invest in the Next Generation 217

Share Your Failures and Successes 219

Remember, Some Relationships Are for a Lifetime, Others for a Season.. 221

Don't Fear Being Used; Fear Not Allowing God to Use You to the Fullest 222

Your Ultimate Reward is Not on Earth; It is Eternity 225

Preface

Welcome to "Thy Kingdom Come," a heartwarming journey into the heart of what it means to build God's Kingdom right here, right now, through the beautiful art of relationship building. This isn't just any book; it's a conversation, a shared journey where we discover the incredible power of connecting with others through what we have in common, our divine purpose, and, most importantly, love.

Picture this book as a friendly guide, walking alongside you, exploring the many layers of forming deep, meaningful connections. It's like having a heart-to-heart chat about how each of us, as proud citizens of the Kingdom, can make a real difference – in our lives, in the lives of others, and in the very fabric of the world, by living out the values and principles that the Kingdom of God holds dear.

Let's start by talking about connections. In "Thy Kingdom Come," we see how our relationships aren't just random meet-ups. They're divine appointments, perfectly orchestrated by God. Imagine, every person you meet is a thread in the vibrant tapestry of your life, and when we approach these relationships with purpose and wisdom from above, they turn into unbreakable bonds that can weather any storm life throws our way.

Now, think about common ground. In a world where differences often take the front seat, this book is your gentle reminder to look for what brings us together. It's like finding those special moments of shared laughter, dreams, and values that remind us of our shared humanity and our collective journey in God's Kingdom. We'll explore stories, Biblical insights, and some really practical tips on how to build bridges, not walls, with those around us.

Purpose – oh, how important that is! "Thy Kingdom Come" is not just about being friendly; it's about being intentional. It's about seeing the big picture, recognizing that our time here is more than just about us. It's a call to align our passions, talents, and daily choices with God's grand plan, turning our ordinary days into extraordinary opportunities for touching lives and making a real difference.

And then there's love. Not just any love, but the kind of love that moves mountains, the love that reflects God's own heart. This book delves into how embracing this love can transform not just our relationships but also us, from the inside out. It's about spreading kindness, patience, and selflessness, and watching them work their magic in our lives and in the world around us.

Finally, "Thy Kingdom Come" doesn't just stop at personal relationships. It paints a bigger picture – a vision of a world where every interaction is a chance to showcase the values of God's Kingdom: peace, justice, and compassion. It's a call to be change-makers, to use our voices and actions to shape a world that mirrors these heavenly principles.

So, are you ready? Ready to embark on this inspiring journey with me? "Thy Kingdom Come" is more than a book – it's a heart-to-heart invitation to be part of something bigger, something beautiful. Together, let's discover the joy of building His Kingdom on earth, one relationship, one conversation, one act of love at a time. Let's start this incredible journey, shall we?

Chapter 1

Introduction to Kingdom Building

This chapter isn't just the beginning of a book; it's the laying of a foundation, the first step in understanding a concept that will transform the way we view and engage in relationships. Here, we delve into the heart of kingdom building, exploring its profound significance and how it fundamentally shapes our interactions with others.

As we embark on this exploration, we start by shedding light on the grand narrative of the Kingdom of God. It's a narrative where Jesus Christ isn't just a historical figure, but the King of Kings, whose teachings and life are the cornerstone of this kingdom. This chapter aims to illuminate how the principles of His Kingdom, when applied, can profoundly influence our everyday relationships. We're talking about relationships that are not just social obligations but divine opportunities to manifest the values of this Kingdom.

In "Introduction to Kingdom Building," we unfold the concept of kingdom building in a way that is accessible and deeply relevant to our daily lives. It's about understanding that our interactions, no matter how small or seemingly insignificant, can have eternal implications. We learn how kingdom building isn't limited to grand gestures or monumental acts; it's often in the simple acts of kindness, understanding, and love that we reflect the heart of our King.

This chapter is an invitation to view our roles in relationships not just as individuals, but as ambassadors of a higher calling. We delve into what it means to be a Kingdom Citizen – living out our God-given purpose and influencing the world around us with the ethos of the Kingdom. This perspective doesn't just change how we connect with others; it redefines our purpose in every interaction, whether in our homes, workplaces, or communities.

As you journey through this chapter, I encourage you to embrace the concept of kingdom building as a foundational element in your relationships. Understand how integrating these Kingdom principles can bring a deeper, more purposeful dimension to your connections with others. Let this be the beginning of a transformative experience, where you see the power of Kingdom Building in shaping a world driven by love, understanding, and divine purpose. Welcome to the foundational journey of Kingdom Building, a journey that promises to redefine your relationships and your role in God's magnificent plan.

Understanding Kingdom Citizenship and Kingdom Building

Imagine for a moment, in the bustling rhythm of our daily lives and amidst the complexities of relationships, that we discover a hidden map. This map isn't made of paper or ink; it's woven through the very fabric of our lives. This map is the profound concept of Kingdom Building, a beacon of hope and direction in a world often clouded by confusion and despair. As Christians, we embark on a journey not in solitude but as integral parts of a grander narrative, one masterfully orchestrated by the King of Kings, Jesus Christ.

Kingdom Citizenship is our identity in this narrative. Think of it as being part of an ancient, royal lineage. Our King, Jesus, speaks of this Kingdom in the Gospel of Matthew (6:33): "But seek first his kingdom and his righteousness, and all these things will be given to you as well." Here, Jesus isn't just offering advice; He's revealing the secret to a life of fulfillment and purpose. Kingdom Citizenship means seeking God's Kingdom above all else, making His values, His teachings, and His love the guiding principles of our lives.

But what is this Kingdom we are part of? It's not a physical realm, but a spiritual kingdom where love reigns supreme, where peace is more than an absence of conflict, and where joy isn't dependent on circumstances. It's a kingdom where relationships are not based on what we can get, but on what we can give. This is Kingdom Building – the act of bringing the atmosphere of heaven to earth, particularly in our relationships.

Consider the story of the Good Samaritan in Luke 10:30-37. Here, Jesus illustrates Kingdom Building through an act of compassion between strangers. The Samaritan, who culturally should have been indifferent, instead embodies Kingdom principles by caring for a wounded man. This story isn't just a lesson in ethics; it's a blueprint for Kingdom Building – a demonstration of God's love in action.

Kingdom Building in relationships is about reflecting God's love in our daily interactions. It's viewing every conversation, every act of kindness, and every challenge as an opportunity to demonstrate the values of the Kingdom. It's about seeking reconciliation over conflict, understanding over judgment, and grace over condemnation.

In 1 Corinthians 13:2, Paul writes, "If I have the gift of prophecy and can fathom all mysteries and all knowledge, and if I have a faith that can move mountains, but do not have love, I am nothing." This powerful statement underscores the essence of Kingdom Building – love. It's a love that transcends human understanding, a love that motivates us to serve, to give, and to build others up.

As you journey through this chapter, imagine yourself as a builder, not with bricks and mortar, but with acts of love, words of encouragement, and deeds of kindness. Understand that your role as a Kingdom Citizen is not a passive one; it's an active participation in a divine mission. You are called to be a light in the darkness, a source of hope and love in a world that desperately needs it. Embrace this calling, and let the principles of Kingdom Citizenship guide your path. Welcome to the journey of understanding Kingdom Citizenship & Kingdom Building – a journey of transforming lives and relationships with the eternal love of God.

Why is Jesus King of Kings and Lord of Lords?

To fully grasp the essence of Kingdom Building, we must journey to the heart of our faith, exploring the majestic role of Jesus Christ as the King of Kings and Lord of Lords. This isn't just a ceremonial title, but a profound truth that sits at the core of the Christian tapestry. In Him, we find the cornerstone of our faith, the ultimate ruler whose authority eclipses all earthly powers. His reign is not one of tyranny or fear, but of righteousness, justice, and a love so deep it transcends human understanding.

Picture a kingdom, not like any earthly realm, but one that stretches beyond the boundaries of time and space. This kingdom isn't governed by the whims of man but by the steadfast, unchangeable nature of God. At the helm is Jesus, whose kingship redefines the very concept of power and authority. In Philippians 2:9-11, Paul writes of Jesus: "Therefore God exalted him to the highest place and gave him the name that is above every name, that at the name of Jesus every knee should bow, in heaven and on earth and under the earth, and every tongue acknowledge that Jesus Christ is Lord, to the glory of God the Father." In these words, we find the acknowledgment of Jesus' ultimate authority and divine rulership.

The significance of Jesus as the King of Kings extends far beyond the spiritual realm; it infiltrates the very fabric of our daily lives, especially in how we build and maintain our relationships. His teachings, parables, and life are not just stories or historical accounts; they are blueprints for a life lived in accordance with the principles of His Kingdom. When Jesus taught us to love our neighbors as ourselves (Mark 12:31), He was laying the foundation for relationships that mirror the heart of His Kingdom.

Imagine living in a world where every interaction is infused with the righteousness, justice, and love that Jesus exemplified. In His dealings with people from all walks of life, Jesus showed what it means to lead with compassion, integrity, and a relentless pursuit of what is right. He dined with sinners, spoke truths that challenged the status quo, and extended mercy where none was expected. In doing so, Jesus illustrated what true kingship looks like – it is servant leadership, it is sacrificial love, and it is transformative grace.

Jesus' role as the King of Kings is more than a testament to His authority over creation; it's a model for us to emulate in our own lives. In John 13:15, after washing His disciples' feet, Jesus said, "I have set you an example that you should do as I have done for you." In this profound act, He demonstrated that true leadership, true kingship, involves humility and serving others – a stark contrast to worldly notions of power and dominion.

As we ponder why Jesus is the King of Kings and Lord of Lords, we are not just acknowledging His sovereignty; we are embracing a way of life that honors and reflects His rulership. It's a commitment to build our relationships on the bedrock of His teachings, to foster connections that are steeped in righteousness, justice, and divine love.

In understanding the kingship of Jesus, we are called to a higher purpose. We are beckoned to live not as subjects to the transient powers of this world, but as citizens of a heavenly Kingdom, where Jesus reigns supreme. This understanding isn't just theological; it's practical, permeating every aspect of our lives, guiding us to live in a manner worthy of our King.

This is the heart of Kingdom Building – living and loving in a way that brings honor to Jesus, the King of Kings and Lord of Lords. As we journey through this exploration, let us be inspired to transform our relationships, our communities, and indeed, our very lives, in light of His glorious kingship. Let us remember that in every act of kindness, in every word of truth, and in every pursuit of justice, we are reflecting the reign of our King, bringing the essence of His Kingdom to a world in need.

What is The Kingdom of God?

In a world bustling with ambitions, desires, and conflicts, there lies a hidden kingdom, not of this world yet intimately intertwined with our every moment. This is the Kingdom of God, often misconceived as a distant, ethereal realm, awaiting us in the afterlife. Yet, this Kingdom is much more present and tangible than many realize; it's a domain where God's will is not just dreamed of but actively pursued and manifested in our daily lives.

To understand the Kingdom of God is to embark on a journey beyond the physical boundaries of our existence. It's to explore a realm where the values of our Creator are lived out in their purest form. Jesus spoke of this Kingdom throughout His ministry. In the Gospel of Luke (17:21), He declares, "The kingdom of God is in your midst." Here, Jesus is not speaking of a future geographical entity; He's revealing a profound truth - the Kingdom of God is here and now, among us, within us.

But what does this mean for us as believers? We are called not just to await the Kingdom's full realization but to actively participate in its unfolding on earth. This isn't a passive waiting; it's an active, vibrant involvement in bringing the ethos of the Kingdom to life in our everyday interactions.

The Kingdom of God is where love reigns supreme. It's a realm where our relationships are governed not by selfish ambition or fleeting emotions but by the selfless, sacrificial love exemplified by Jesus Christ. In John 13:34, Jesus commands, "As I have loved you, so you must love one another." In this, He sets the standard of love that defines the Kingdom - a love that serves, forgives, and uplifts.

Imagine a world where every relationship is a reflection of this divine love. Where conflicts are resolved not with bitterness or resentment, but with forgiveness and understanding. This is the essence of the Kingdom of God - a place where the fruits of the Spirit, as mentioned in Galatians 5:22-23 - love, joy, peace, forbearance, kindness, goodness, faithfulness, gentleness, and self-control - are not just ideals but living realities.

The Kingdom of God is also a domain of peace. In Matthew 5:9, Jesus blesses the peacemakers, calling them "children of God." Here, He is inviting us to be architects of peace in our relationships and communities. This peace is not the absence of conflict but the presence of righteousness, justice, and compassion. It's an active pursuit to create harmony, understanding, and mutual respect among people.

Service is another hallmark of the Kingdom. In Mark 10:45, Jesus tells us that He came not to be served, but to serve. This model of servant leadership is at the core of the Kingdom's values. It's about putting others' needs above our own, about finding joy in the act of giving, and about being the hands and feet of Jesus in a world that desperately needs His touch.

But the Kingdom of God is not just about how we treat others; it's also about personal transformation. It's a call to live lives that are radically different from the norms of this world, lives that are a testament to the transformative power of God's love. In Romans 12:2, Paul urges us not to conform to the pattern of this world, but to be transformed by the renewing of our minds. This transformation is the essence of Kingdom living - it's about aligning our thoughts, actions, and desires with God's will.

The Kingdom of God, then, is not a far-off or abstract concept. It's a living, breathing reality that we are invited to participate in every day. It's about seeing our relationships as platforms to demonstrate Kingdom values, about transforming our workplaces, homes, and communities with the ethos of this Kingdom. It's about living in such a way that our lives bear witness to the reality of God's reign.

As you contemplate the Kingdom of God, remember it's not just about awaiting a future glory; it's about embodying and reflecting the glory of God here and now. It's about being agents of His love, peace, and righteousness in a world that longs for these very things. The Kingdom of God is among us, within us, and through us, manifesting in every act of kindness, every word of truth, and every gesture of love. As believers, we are not just subjects of this Kingdom; we are active participants, co-creators with Christ in bringing the beauty, justice, and love of His Kingdom to every corner of our world.

How and Why Are True Christians Adopted into The Family of God?

In the grand narrative of humanity, there is a transformation so profound, so life-altering, that it changes the very essence of our being. This transformation is the adoption into God's family, a spiritual journey that shifts our identity from being merely God's creation to becoming His beloved children. This adoption is not a mere change of status; it's a rebirth, a complete realignment of our purpose, identity, and destiny.

To understand how this adoption occurs, we must first look to the central figure of our faith, Jesus Christ. In Him, we find the key to this profound mystery. John 1:12 tells us, "Yet to all who did receive him, to those who believed in his name, he gave the right to become children of God." It's a simple yet radical concept: by placing our faith in Jesus, by receiving Him into our hearts, we are given the incredible privilege of becoming God's children. This isn't a reward for good behavior or a title earned by deeds; it's a gift, freely given out of God's boundless love.

But why does God adopt us into His family? The answer lies in His very nature. 1 John 4:8 reveals that "God is love." His desire to adopt us isn't born out of necessity or obligation; it's an expression of His infinite love. In this divine love story, we see a Father who longed for a family, who created humanity not as distant beings to rule over but as children to love, cherish, and nurture.

Picture a family reunion, where every member, regardless of their past, is welcomed with open arms, where stories are shared, laughter rings out, and love is the underlying theme. This is the picture of

God's family. In this family, there are no outcasts, no forgotten members. Each one of us, by virtue of our faith in Christ, is given a place at the table, a room in the house.

The significance of this adoption is monumental. In Romans 8:15-17, Paul writes, "The Spirit you received does not make you slaves, so that you live in fear again; rather, the Spirit you received brought about your adoption to sonship. And by him we cry, 'Abba, Father.'" Here, Paul is painting a picture of intimacy, security, and belonging. As adopted children, we are not slaves living in fear; we are sons and daughters who can call God 'Abba' – a term of endearment, akin to 'Daddy'. This is a radical shift from a religion of fear to a relationship of love.

This adoption also redefines our relationships with others. As members of God's family, our connections with fellow believers go deeper than mere friendship or fellowship; they are bonds of a shared spiritual lineage. Galatians 6:10 encourages us, "Therefore, as we have opportunity, let us do good to all people, especially to those who belong to the family of believers." Our relationships are no longer defined by social status, race, or background; they are defined by the mutual recognition that we are siblings in Christ.

Our adoption into God's family also brings a new sense of purpose and destiny. In Ephesians 2:10, Paul tells us, "For we are God's handiwork, created in Christ Jesus to do good works, which God prepared in advance for us to do." As God's children, we are not aimlessly wandering through life; we are walking in a destiny prepared for us by our Heavenly Father. Our lives, our talents, our dreams – all are part of God's grand design, a tapestry of His making.

Being part of God's family also means we are part of a bigger story – a story of redemption, hope, and love. In this family, our struggles, our victories, our joys, and our pains are shared. We are not isolated islands but a connected body, supporting and uplifting one another. In this divine family, we find a place of refuge, a source of strength, and a wellspring of inspiration.

In this adoption, we also find our true identity. In a world where identity is often tied to fleeting things like career, relationships, or possessions, our status as God's children offers a firm, unshakeable foundation. 1 Peter 2:9 reminds us, "But you are a chosen people, a royal priesthood, a holy nation, God's special possession, that you may declare the praises of him who called you out of darkness into his wonderful light." This is who we are – chosen, royal, holy, and special in the eyes of God.

Our adoption into God's family is not the end of the journey; it's the beginning. It's the starting point of a life lived in the fullness of God's love, a life where every relationship is an opportunity to demonstrate the love, grace, and mercy we have received. It's a call to live not as products of our past but as pioneers of our destiny, not as victims of circumstance but as victors in Christ.

As we embrace our identity as God's adopted children, let us walk in the assurance of His love, the confidence of our calling, and the joy of our divine kinship. Let us view our relationships as extensions of this heavenly family, where every interaction is imbued with the grace and love of our Father. In this family, we find our true purpose, our true identity, and our true home. Welcome to the family of God – a family of love, a family of purpose, a family for eternity.

What is our God-Given Purpose as Kingdom Citizens?

In the grand narrative of humanity, each of us plays a unique role, intricately linked to a purpose far greater than our individual ambitions. As citizens of God's Kingdom, we are called to a life that transcends personal goals and societal norms. This calling is not merely a duty; it is an embodiment of our identity as ambassadors of Christ.

To fully embrace our God-given purpose, imagine a world where each interaction, each word, and each choice is a reflection of Christ's love and truth. This vision captures the essence of a Kingdom Citizen's life – a life where ordinary moments become divine opportunities to showcase the reality of God's Kingdom. Our daily encounters are not just routine; they are chances to bring healing, understanding, and unity to places scarred by division and strife.

Being an ambassador of Christ is a dynamic and living commitment. According to 2 Corinthians 5:20, "We are therefore Christ's ambassadors, as though God were making his appeal through us." We carry the profound responsibility and honor of representing Christ in every aspect of our lives. In every conversation and action, we have the chance to be His voice, hands, and heart in a world in need of His touch.

Living out this purpose means that our words are not merely our own but echoes of divine truth and encouragement. Our actions stem from a wellspring of compassion, integrity, and love. Our choices and decisions are aligned with God's will, contributing to the expansion and enrichment of His Kingdom.

Consider the Good Samaritan's story in Luke 10:25-37. Jesus uses this parable to illustrate the active, compassionate life of a Kingdom Citizen. The Samaritan's actions crossed societal barriers to help a stranger, embodying the Kingdom's values. We are called to similar actions of compassion and kindness, especially towards those who are often ignored or undervalued in our communities.

As peacemakers, we embrace the blessing bestowed in Matthew 5:9: "Blessed are the peacemakers, for they will be called children of God." Our role is to diffuse conflict, not to exacerbate it, bringing the peace of Christ into every challenging situation.

We are also called to be lights in a world often shrouded in darkness. In Matthew 5:14-16, Jesus tells us we are the light of the world, a beacon set on a hill, impossible to hide. This imagery speaks of our influence and responsibility to illuminate the world with the principles and love of the Kingdom.

Our primary pursuit, as instructed by Jesus in Matthew 6:33, is to "seek first his kingdom and his righteousness." This pursuit is the heartbeat of a Kingdom Citizen, prioritizing the advancement of God's Kingdom over worldly achievements or recognition.

Our role as Kingdom Citizens extends beyond individual pursuits. We are part of a broader, interconnected community of believers. In this community, we find strength, encouragement, and mutual growth. Our interactions are not limited to social engagements but are opportunities to spiritually enrich and support one another.

This calling to Kingdom Citizenship is not restricted to the confines of church walls. It permeates every aspect of our lives – family, workplace, community, and beyond. In each of these areas, we bring the transformative values of the Kingdom, impacting the world in Christ's name.

Embracing this purpose leads to a deep sense of fulfillment, peace, and joy. It transcends earthly satisfaction, anchoring us in a mission that contributes to something eternal and much more significant than our individual stories.

As Kingdom Citizens, our lives are a continuous journey of divine encounters and opportunities to express God's love. It's a life graced by the Holy Spirit, driven by an unyielding desire to see His Kingdom manifest on earth as it is in heaven. This is our purpose and our greatest calling – to live each day as a living testament to His love, grace, and sovereign reign. Let us wholeheartedly embrace this calling, making every day count for His glory and the advancement of His Kingdom.

How Do We Accomplish Our Purpose?

In the grand and unfolding story of God's Kingdom, each of us holds a vital role, a purpose imbued by our Creator. This purpose is not a mere task to be completed; it's a calling to live a life that echoes the heart of God. But how do we accomplish this high calling? It's a journey that requires more than human will or effort; it requires a conscious, daily commitment to live out the principles of God's Kingdom, guided and empowered by His Spirit.

Imagine setting sail on an ancient sea, navigating by the stars. This journey is similar to our quest to accomplish our God-given purpose. The stars in our journey are the timeless principles laid out in Scripture, guiding us through the tumultuous waters of life. Our compass is our ongoing, deepening relationship with God, nurtured through prayer, meditation on His Word, and heartfelt worship. These practices are not religious obligations but lifelines that keep us connected to our Divine Navigator.

Consider the words of Jesus in John 15:5, "I am the vine; you are the branches. If you remain in me and I in you, you will bear much fruit; apart from me you can do nothing." Here, Jesus illustrates our dependence on Him to fulfill our purpose. Like branches connected to the vine, drawing nourishment and life, we too must remain intimately connected to Christ. This connection is the source of our strength, wisdom, and direction.

In our relationships, accomplishing our purpose means choosing love over indifference. It's about seeing every person, not as a stranger or an opponent, but as a fellow traveler on this journey of life. Love, as described in 1 Corinthians 13:4-7, is patient, kind, and devoid of envy or pride. This love is not passive; it's active, seeking the best for others, bearing all things, believing all things, hoping all things, and enduring all things.

Choosing forgiveness over grudges is another cornerstone in accomplishing our purpose. Ephesians 4:32 urges us to "be kind and compassionate to one another, forgiving each other, just as in Christ God forgave you." Forgiveness is not an approval of wrongdoing; it's a liberation from the bondage of bitterness. It's a powerful declaration that we are not defined by the hurts we have suffered, but by the grace we have received and are willing to extend.

Unity over division is a clarion call for Kingdom Citizens. In a world often fractured by discord and strife, we are called to be bridge-builders. Ephesians 2:14 reminds us that Christ is our peace, who has broken down the dividing wall of hostility. Our role is to continue this work of reconciliation, creating spaces where understanding and mutual respect can flourish.

Living out our purpose also means being salt and light in the world (Matthew 5:13-16). As salt, we are called to enhance and preserve the goodness in the world. As light, we are to illuminate the dark corners of injustice, despair, and hopelessness. In every sphere of our lives – whether in our families, workplaces, communities, or beyond – we have the opportunity to bring the flavor of the Kingdom and to shine the light of Christ's love and truth.

Spiritual disciplines such as prayer, fasting, and studying Scripture are not mere rituals; they are tools that sharpen us, aligning our hearts and minds with God's will. Through prayer, we communicate with God, express our dependence on Him, and align our desires with His. Fasting is a powerful means of humbling ourselves before God, reminding us of our frailty and His sufficiency. Studying Scripture immerses us in the narrative of God's work in the world, equipping us with wisdom and insight for our daily lives.

Serving others is another critical aspect of accomplishing our purpose. Galatians 5:13 encourages us, "serve one another humbly in love." Service is the hallmark of the Kingdom – it's about putting the needs of others above our own, finding joy in the act of giving rather than receiving.

Worship, both communal and personal, is vital in accomplishing our purpose. It's in these moments of worship that we are reminded of who God is and who we are in Him. Worship reorients our perspective, enabling us to see beyond our circumstances and focus on the eternal.

As we journey to accomplish our God-given purpose, let us remember that it's not by our strength or ability but by God's Spirit (Zechariah 4:6). It's a daily surrendering of our will to His, a constant striving to reflect His love and grace in a world in desperate need of His touch.

To accomplish our purpose as Kingdom Citizens, we must be grounded in our relationship with God, live out His principles in our relationships, and actively participate in His transformative work in the world. It's a journey that requires faith, perseverance, and a heart attuned to God's voice.1

Thy Kingdom Come

In the intricate dance of life, where each step and turn weaves the story of our existence, there lies a deeper rhythm, a melody that resonates with the divine. This rhythm is the heartbeat of "Thy Kingdom Come," a prayer, a declaration, and a commitment to live out the values of God's Kingdom here on earth. As we journey through this narrative, we find ourselves entwined in a quest not just of personal ambition but of celestial significance. Our relationships, those delicate threads that connect us to one another, become the very fabric through which God's Kingdom is revealed and His purposes are fulfilled.

Imagine a world where every encounter is laden with the potential to echo the values of heaven. This is the realm of Kingdom Citizens, individuals who, in the ordinariness of their lives, choose to enact an extraordinary mission. It's a world where the common coffee shop becomes a sanctuary of encouragement, the bustling streets a canvas for acts of kindness, and the quiet moments at home an altar of forgiveness and grace.

In this world, the story of Anna and John unfolds. They met in the unlikeliest of places, their paths crossing in a small community garden. Anna, a retired teacher, found solace in the garden's tranquility, a respite from her loneliness. John, a busy executive, stumbled upon the garden in search of quiet amidst the chaos of his life. Their friendship blossomed like the flowers around them, rooted in shared conversations, laughter, and eventually, prayers.

Through their interactions, the garden became more than a patch of green in a concrete city. It transformed into a testament of God's Kingdom on earth. Each seed they planted, each weed they pulled, mirrored the work they did in their hearts - planting seeds of hope, uprooting bitterness, and nurturing the tender shoots of a newfound faith.

In another chapter of this narrative, we find Sarah, a young nurse whose compassion extended beyond the hospital wards. Her encounters with patients were not mere professional duties; they were divine appointments to demonstrate the love and care of Christ. When she held the hands of the sick, she did more than offer physical comfort; she conveyed a message of hope and peace. Her work was her ministry, her service a living prayer of "Thy Kingdom Come."

In the heart of the city, there was Michael, a businessman known for his integrity and fairness. His office was a beacon of light, a place where honesty reigned and respect was the currency. Michael's success was not measured by his wealth but by the trust and esteem he earned. His leadership was a daily embodiment of "Thy Kingdom Come," as he strove to reflect Christ's love and justice in every deal and decision.

These stories, and countless others, weave the narrative of "Thy Kingdom Come." They are tales of ordinary people who chose to live out their God-given purpose, transforming their relationships into conduits of God's grace. Their lives were not without challenges, their paths not without obstacles, but their commitment to live as Kingdom Citizens never wavered.

In this journey, forgiveness became a powerful theme, a recurrent melody that harmonized relationships. Like the story of Emma, who forgave her estranged brother, extending an olive branch that mended years of hurt and misunderstanding. Her act of forgiveness was a ripple in the pond, inspiring others in her community to let go of grudges and embrace reconciliation.

Humility and service wove through these narratives as golden threads. Individuals like Thomas, a volunteer at a local shelter, exemplified this. He served not for recognition but out of a genuine desire to reflect God's love. His humility was evident in the way he interacted with each person he met, seeing them not as projects but as precious souls.

Each of these stories, a tapestry of lives intertwined by divine purpose, reflects the essence of "Thy Kingdom Come." It's a kingdom where love reigns supreme, where forgiveness bridges the widest gaps, and where humble service uplifts the downtrodden. It's a kingdom manifest not in grandiose gestures but in the daily acts of kindness, compassion, and love.

As we ponder the journey of "Thy Kingdom Come," let us be inspired by these narratives. Let us recognize that our relationships are more than mere connections; they are sacred opportunities to display the love, grace, and truth of God. Every interaction is a chance to advance His Kingdom, to bring a piece of heaven to earth, to live out the prayer that Christ Himself taught us.

In this world, the prayer "Thy Kingdom come" becomes more than a line in Scripture; it becomes a way of life, a pulse that drives our every action and interaction. Let us then commit to this journey, to building relationships that honor our King, advance His Kingdom, and bring glory to His name. Let every word we speak, every bond we form, every challenge we overcome be a living testament to the prayer "Thy Kingdom come," echoing in the corridors of time and resonating in the chambers of eternity.

Chapter 2

The Power of Commonalities

Embark with me on a profound exploration in this second chapter, where we dive deep into the heart of what connects us – the powerful, often underappreciated, world of commonalities. Here, we don't just skim the surface of superficial similarities; we plunge into the depths of shared values, dreams, and goals, discovering the immense strength and undeniable beauty that lie within.

Imagine a world where differences in appearance, background, and culture are not barriers but gateways to richer, more meaningful connections. In this world, we recognize that our true bond lies in what we hold dear in our hearts, in the dreams that ignite our souls, and the goals that drive our lives forward. It's a world where shared spiritual journeys and Kingdom-focused aspirations form the bedrock of our relationships, creating a unity that transcends external disparities.

In this chapter, we explore the transformative power of commonalities. It's a journey through stories and insights, revealing how our common goals and values are not just points of agreement but potent catalysts for deep and lasting connections. These commonalities act as lighthouses, guiding us through the fog of our differences, helping us find and connect with others who walk a similar path, who share the same heartbeat for God's Kingdom.

Think of the early church, as described in Acts 2:44-47, where believers "had everything in common." This wasn't just about sharing material possessions; it was about sharing life, a unified vision, and a collective mission. They were bound together not by law or obligation but by a shared love for Christ and a common goal to spread His message. This powerful unity led to unprecedented growth, both in numbers and in spiritual depth.

Reflect on the lives of great men and women of faith, whose relationships were forged not merely by circumstance but by a shared commitment to God's work. Consider the friendships of Paul and Timothy, Ruth and Naomi, David and Jonathan – relationships that illustrate how common spiritual objectives and values can create bonds that withstand the toughest of trials.

In our contemporary world, the need for such connections has never been greater. Amidst the noise of division and the clamor of conflicting ideologies, finding and nurturing relationships with those who share our spiritual journey is both a refuge and a source of strength. These relationships encourage us to persevere in faith, inspire us to live out our God-given purpose, and provide a support system that uplifts and sustains us.

But how do we identify and cultivate these commonalities in a world that often emphasizes what sets us apart? This chapter delves into practical, actionable strategies to discover and build on shared values, dreams, and aspirations. It's about learning to ask the right questions, to listen deeply, and to observe the subtleties that reveal what truly matters to those we encounter.

Moreover, we explore the beauty that emerges when commonalities in relationships are celebrated and nurtured. These connections bring a sense of belonging, understanding, and mutual respect, which are essential in building a strong community of believers. They foster an environment where we can grow spiritually, challenge each other in love, and work together towards the advancement of God's Kingdom.

As Kingdom citizens, recognizing and leveraging our commonalities is not just beneficial; it's essential. It aligns with Jesus' prayer for unity among His followers in John 17:21-23, where He prays that we may be one, just as He and the Father are one. This unity is a testimony to the world of God's love and power.

In this chapter, we don't just acknowledge the power of commonalities; we learn to actively seek it out and let it flourish in our lives. It's a call to look beyond the external and connect on a deeper, more spiritual level. By doing so, we not only enrich our own lives but also contribute to the strength and health of the broader body of Christ.

So, let's journey together through "The Power of Commonalities," exploring, discovering, and embracing the shared values, dreams, and goals that bind us. In doing so, we forge relationships that are not only enduring and fulfilling but also instrumental in bringing to fruition the beautiful, powerful vision of God's Kingdom on earth.

We Must Be Deliberate and Intentional About Our Kingdom Associations

In the quest for Kingdom Building, the connections we create play a pivotal role. Our journey through this chapter explores the depth and resilience of relationships rooted in shared values, dreams, and goals. Here, we learn the significance of being deliberate and intentional in cultivating Kingdom associations, transcending beyond mere external differences to uncover the profound unity we share in Christ.

Picture yourself walking through a dense forest, where each tree represents a potential relationship. This forest is vast, with a variety of trees – some providing shade and shelter, others bearing fruit, and yet others standing tall and strong. Like these trees, the relationships we seek should offer shelter in times of storm, nourishment for our growth, and strength to stand firm in our faith. The scripture in Proverbs 12:26 guides us: "The righteous choose their friends carefully, but the way of the wicked leads them astray." This is a reminder to us that in our quest for connections, discernment is key.

Take, for instance, the story of Emma and Lucas. Both were active in their local church but came from different walks of life. Emma, a veteran in community service and deeply rooted in her faith, met Lucas, who was just beginning his spiritual journey, during a church outreach program. Initially, their differences seemed more apparent than their similarities. However, as they worked together, a shared passion for service and a common desire to embody Christ's love in their actions became evident. Their relationship, built on these shared values, flourished, illustrating the strength that lies in Kingdom-focused connections.

Envision a world where such intentional relationships are the cornerstone of our social interactions. In this world, our friendships and associations are not a matter of chance but are carefully chosen and nurtured, much like a gardener who selects plants that will thrive together. These relationships become a reflection of the fruitful bond Jesus describes in John 15:5, "I am the vine; you are the branches. If you remain in me and I in you, you will bear much fruit; apart from me you can do nothing." Remaining connected to Christ and to fellow believers with similar values and visions enhances our capacity to impact the world positively.

Embracing diversity within the body of Christ is a vital aspect of forming intentional Kingdom associations. Like a vibrant mosaic, the beauty and strength of the body of Christ lie in its varied and unique pieces. In 1 Corinthians 12:12-14, Paul speaks of the body of Christ as being made up of many parts, each with its distinct role yet part of a unified whole. This diversity is not a source of division but a foundation for a stronger, more harmonious community, each member contributing their unique gifts and talents to the collective mission.

Building intentional Kingdom associations also involves fostering environments of mutual growth and encouragement. As stated in Romans 14:19, "Let us therefore make every effort to do what leads to peace and to mutual edification." Our relationships should not only comfort and support us; they should also challenge us to grow, to sharpen each other, and to inspire greater acts of love and kindness.

This chapter is about more than finding individuals who share our beliefs and values; it's about actively building a community where mutual respect, love, and growth are central. It's about understanding that our choices in relationships can profoundly influence our personal and spiritual development, and ultimately, our effectiveness in God's Kingdom.

In committing to be deliberate and intentional about our Kingdom associations, we also recognize the importance of seeking God's guidance. Through prayer and the leading of the Holy Spirit, we can discern which relationships align with God's will and purpose for our lives. United in our love for Christ and dedication to His Kingdom, our relationships transcend mere friendships; they become a dynamic force for God's transformative work in the world.

As we close this section, let us embrace the call to seek and nurture those connections that resonate with our Kingdom mission. Let every relationship we cultivate be a reflection of the unity and love found in Christ, a conscious effort to contribute to the building of God's Kingdom, one intentional connection at a time.

Intentionally Search for Those That Are Like-minded

In the vibrant landscape of Kingdom Building, the pursuit of meaningful relationships takes us on a journey marked by intention and purpose. This quest, centered around intentionally searching for those that are like-minded, is akin to a mariner setting sail, seeking lands that resonate with the desires of his heart. It's a journey not of solitude, but of camaraderie, where finding fellow believers with shared values, aspirations, and commitments to the principles of God's Kingdom, shapes the course of our spiritual voyage.

Imagine a world where each believer is a beacon of light, shining forth their faith and values. In this world, our task is to navigate towards these beacons, seeking those whose light complements and enhances our own. The scripture in Amos 3:3 asks, "Do two walk together unless they have agreed to do so?" This verse underscores the importance of finding unity in purpose and vision. Our quest is not simply to find companions for our journey but to find fellow travelers who share the same destination – the advancement of God's Kingdom on earth.

The story of Daniel and his companions in Babylon exemplifies this quest. Thrust into a foreign land, they sought each other out, bound by their commitment to uphold the decrees of their God amidst an alien culture. In Daniel 1:8, we see Daniel's resolve not to defile himself with the royal food and wine, a conviction shared by his friends. Their like-mindedness created a bond of strength and mutual support that enabled them to thrive and witness to the power of God in a foreign land.

Now, consider the journey of Lydia, a seller of purple cloth in the city of Philippi, as narrated in Acts 16. When she met Paul and his companions, there was an instant connection, rooted in their shared faith. Lydia's heart was open to Paul's message, and this like-mindedness led her to not only embrace the gospel but also to extend hospitality to these messengers of Christ. Here, we see how like-mindedness extends beyond shared beliefs to shared actions, fostering a community where the love of Christ is tangibly expressed.

Our quest for like-minded individuals is not merely about comfort or compatibility; it's about creating a synergistic environment where spiritual growth, mutual support, and Kingdom advancement flourish. It's about recognizing that "iron sharpens iron" as stated in Proverbs 27:17. In our interactions with those who share our Kingdom-focused aspirations, we find ourselves sharpened, challenged, and inspired to delve deeper into our faith.

In seeking like-minded individuals, we embrace the richness of diversity within the body of Christ. Like a harmonious orchestra, each member brings a unique tone, yet all play in concert under the same score – the principles of God's Kingdom. Ephesians 4:16 speaks of the body of Christ being joined and held together by every supporting ligament, growing and building itself up in love, as each part does its work. In our pursuit of like-minded companions, we discover that unity in purpose does not negate individual uniqueness but rather celebrates and utilizes it for the collective good.

Intentionally seeking like-minded believers also means being proactive in our relationships. It's about venturing into our communities, churches, and places of fellowship with a discerning heart, guided by the Holy Spirit. It's about engaging in conversations, participating in activities, and immersing ourselves in environments where the principles of God's Kingdom are upheld and cherished.

Moreover, this journey involves a commitment to nurture and invest in these relationships. Like the parable of the sower in Matthew 13, we must sow our time, energy, and resources into fertile ground – relationships where the Word of God can grow and yield a hundredfold. This investment is not just for our personal edification but for the strengthening of the wider body of Christ.

Our quest for like-minded companions is, ultimately, a reflection of our desire to emulate Christ. In His earthly ministry, Jesus sought out and surrounded Himself with disciples who shared His commitment to God's will. Together, they formed a fellowship where teachings were imparted, faith was strengthened, and the groundwork for the early Church was laid.

In closing, the search for like-minded individuals is a vital aspect of our Kingdom journey. It's about aligning ourselves with those who echo our spiritual values and aspirations, creating a united front in the face of challenges and a powerful force for Kingdom advancement. Let us, therefore, embark on this quest with intention and purpose, trusting that as we seek these relationships, we are not only building a community of believers but also actively participating in the unfolding of God's glorious Kingdom on earth.

Listen to the Ideas of Others

In the journey of Kingdom Building, the art of listening plays a vital, often unsung role. It's a practice that transforms our interactions, turning mere exchanges into rich, collaborative conversations. This chapter delves into the significance of actively listening to the ideas of others, a practice deeply rooted in the values of God's Kingdom. In God's diverse family, every voice has value, every insight bears potential, and every perspective contributes to a fuller understanding of His will and ways.

Picture a grand symphony orchestra. Each instrument, while distinct in sound and style, contributes to the harmony of the piece. The conductor, with a keen ear, listens intently to each section, ensuring that every note contributes to the symphony's overall beauty. In the same way, the body of Christ is composed of diverse individuals, each carrying unique melodies of insights and experiences. As members of this body, our role is akin to that of the conductor, tuning our ears to listen to the diverse ideas and perspectives of our brothers and sisters.

Consider the story of Mary and Martha in Luke 10:38-42. While Martha was preoccupied with serving, Mary chose to sit at Jesus' feet, listening to His words. In this scenario, we see the value that Jesus places on listening. Mary's choice to listen intently to Jesus' teachings was commended, for in her listening, she received wisdom and understanding that service alone could not impart.

Now, imagine a community where listening is the norm – a place where conversations are not battlegrounds for supremacy of opinion but fertile grounds for learning and growth. In such a community, the ideas of others are not threats but treasures, bringing varied hues of understanding and wisdom. Proverbs 18:13 teaches us, "To answer before listening – that is folly and shame." In Kingdom Building, listening becomes an act of humility and respect, acknowledging that God speaks and works through each of His children.

In actively listening to others, we foster a culture of respect and unity. It's about giving space for different voices to be heard, for different experiences to be shared. This practice is essential in a world where the clamor of conflicting voices often drowns out the still, small voice of wisdom. By valuing the contributions of others, we build a community where every member feels valued, heard, and understood.

Listening to the ideas of others also enhances collaboration and mutual edification. In the early church, as narrated in Acts 15, we witness a critical moment where the apostles and elders gathered to discuss the issue of Gentile believers. It was through careful listening, discussion, and the guidance of the Holy Spirit that they reached a consensus, a decision that would shape the future of the Church. This episode highlights the power of collective wisdom gleaned through attentive listening.

Moreover, in the practice of listening, we echo the heart of Christ. Jesus' ministry was marked by moments where He listened to the needs, questions, and pleas of those around Him. His responses were not just based on divine insight but were also informed by His attentive listening to the hearts of people.

This is not just about the act of listening; it's about cultivating an attitude of openness and receptivity. It's about recognizing that our personal perspectives are limited and that in the multitude of counselors, there is wisdom, as stated in Proverbs 11:14. In the context of Kingdom Building, listening becomes a tool for harmony, a means to weave the diverse threads of individual insights into a cohesive tapestry of collective wisdom.

As we progress in our Kingdom journey, let us embrace the discipline of listening. Let us create spaces where the ideas of others are not only heard but also valued and considered. In doing so, we build a stronger, more unified body of Christ, capable of reflecting His love, wisdom, and grace to a world in need.

Listening to the ideas of others is more than a courtesy; it is a critical component of Kingdom Building. It is an acknowledgment of the varied ways God speaks to and through His people. By practicing intentional listening, we open ourselves to broader understanding, deeper connections, and more effective collaboration in our collective pursuit of advancing God's Kingdom. Let every conversation be an opportunity to learn, every dialogue a chance to grow, and every interaction a step towards a more united and effective body of Christ.

Be Open to Sharing Your Ideas with Others as God Leads

Every believer carries within them a treasure trove of ideas, experiences, and revelations bestowed by God. These are not mere personal assets; they are gifts meant to be shared, seeds destined to be sown into the lives of others. As we journey through the path of faith, being open to sharing our ideas and visions as God leads is not just an act of contribution; it is a pivotal form of service, a vital piece in the puzzle of communal growth and edification in Christ.

Picture a great banquet, where each guest brings a unique dish to the table. The richness of the feast lies not only in the variety of dishes but in the act of sharing. Each dish contributes to a more fulfilling and enjoyable meal, just as each of our ideas and visions, when shared, contribute to a richer, more diverse understanding of God's Kingdom. The apostle Paul, in his letter to the Corinthians, aptly describes this concept in 1 Corinthians 14:26, "Each of you has a hymn, or a word of instruction, a revelation, a tongue, or an interpretation. Everything must be done so that the church may be built up." This scripture is a clarion call for believers to bring forth their God-given insights and revelations, not for personal glory but for the edification of the Body of Christ.

The story of Joseph in Genesis is a profound illustration of the impact of sharing God-given visions. Joseph, through his God-given ability to interpret dreams, not only saved Egypt from famine but also preserved the lineage through which the Messiah would come. His willingness to share his insights, even in less than ideal circumstances, showcases the transformative power of openly communicating the visions God places in our hearts.

Similarly, consider the account of Esther. Positioned by God in the Persian court, Esther was initially hesitant to share her concerns with the king regarding Haman's plot against her people. However, guided by Mordecai's wisdom and spurred by the realization of her divine appointment, Esther courageously shared her plea, ultimately saving her people from destruction. Her story exemplifies how sharing our ideas and insights, particularly in moments of crisis, can have far-reaching and life-saving implications.

In the New Testament, we encounter Priscilla and Aquila, a couple who shared their understanding of the gospel with Apollos, a learned man who was eloquent in scriptures but knew only the baptism of John. In Acts 18:26, we read, "They invited him to their home and explained to him the way of God more adequately."

Through their willingness to share their understanding, they equipped Apollos to be a more effective minister of the gospel.

Our openness to sharing should be fueled not by a desire for validation or dominance but by a sincere intention to contribute to the collective growth of the church. In the book of Proverbs 27:17, we find the wisdom, "As iron sharpens iron, so one person sharpens another." Our shared ideas and insights act as sharpening tools, refining and enhancing each other's understanding and faith.

However, sharing our ideas and visions requires a heart attuned to God's timing and guidance. It's not about offloading every thought or revelation that crosses our minds but about discerning what is beneficial, timely, and edifying. Ephesians 4:29 instructs, "Do not let any unwholesome talk come out of your mouths, but only what is helpful for building others up according to their needs, that it may benefit those who listen." This scripture is a guiding principle, reminding us to share in ways that uplift and encourage others in their walk with Christ.

The act of sharing our ideas also fosters a culture of mutual respect and collaboration within the Body of Christ. It breaks down the walls of isolation and individualism, creating a vibrant community where ideas flow freely, and wisdom is multiplied. Just as the early church in Acts 2:44-47 shared everything they had, so we are called to share not just our material possessions but also our spiritual insights and revelations.

Sharing our ideas is also an act of vulnerability, a demonstration of trust in our fellow believers. It's an acknowledgment that we are part of a larger body, each member valuable and necessary. As we open our hearts and minds to share, we also open the door for others to contribute to our growth, creating a reciprocal cycle of edification.

In embracing the call to be open to sharing our ideas as God leads, we also realize the importance of doing so in love and humility. It's about recognizing that our insights are not superior but are part of a larger mosaic of God's revelation to His church. 1 Peter 4:10-11 encourages us, "Each of you should use whatever gift you have received to serve others, as faithful stewards of God's grace in its various forms."

Embrace Those Outside Your Immediate Circle

In the rich and varied landscape of building God's Kingdom, our journey isn't confined to the familiar territories of our immediate social circles. This part of our spiritual expedition challenges us to venture beyond our comfort zones, to extend the hand of fellowship to those who may not walk our regular paths. This venture of reaching out to individuals from different backgrounds, cultures, and experiences is a critical aspect of embodying the Kingdom of God. It's about reflecting the unconditional love of Christ and demonstrating the unity He yearns to see in His Church. By widening our embrace, we acknowledge and celebrate the magnificent diversity that God has woven into the fabric of His creation.

Imagine a vast garden, lush and flourishing, with a variety of plants and flowers. Each plant, though different in color, shape, and size, contributes to the garden's beauty and diversity. The Kingdom of God is much like this garden – diverse, inclusive, and rich with a variety of experiences, backgrounds, and cultures. As believers, we are called to appreciate and embrace this diversity, recognizing that every individual is a unique creation, beautifully crafted in the image of God.

The story of the Good Samaritan, as told by Jesus in Luke 10:25-37, is a profound illustration of this call. In this parable, the Samaritan, who was culturally and religiously different from the injured Jewish man, didn't hesitate to offer help. His actions broke the barriers of ethnic and cultural prejudices, demonstrating the kind of love and acceptance that defines the Kingdom of God. This parable challenges us to follow suit, to extend our hands and hearts to those who are outside our immediate circle, understanding that the love of Christ knows no boundaries.

Consider also the early church, as depicted in the book of Acts. In Acts 10, we read the story of Peter and Cornelius. Peter, a Jew, initially struggled with the idea of associating with Gentiles. However, through a vision from God, he understood that the Gospel was not just for the Jews but for all people, irrespective of their ethnic background. His subsequent meeting with Cornelius, a Roman centurion, marked a significant turning point in the spread of the Gospel, showcasing the inclusivity and diversity at the heart of God's Kingdom.

Embracing those outside our immediate circles is not always comfortable or easy. It challenges our preconceptions, pushes our boundaries, and often requires us to step into the unknown. Yet, it is in these very acts of stretching and reaching out that we experience the fullness of God's love and the true essence of the church. Galatians 3:28 reminds us, "There is neither Jew nor Greek, slave nor free, male nor female, for you are all one in Christ Jesus." This scripture is a powerful reminder that in Christ, our differences are not divisive but are elements that enrich and strengthen our collective identity as the body of Christ.

Reaching out to those outside our immediate circles also enhances our understanding and appreciation of the vastness of God's work. Each person's story is a unique testimony of God's grace and power. By embracing these diverse stories, we not only broaden our perspectives but also deepen our appreciation for the myriad ways God works in people's lives.

Moreover, by welcoming those from different backgrounds and experiences into our lives and communities, we become living embodiments of Christ's love. We reflect a Kingdom that is not marked by exclusivity or homogeneity but by a love that transcends cultural, ethnic, and social barriers. In doing so, we become catalysts for unity and reconciliation, both within the church and in the broader world.

Embracing those outside our immediate circles is an essential aspect of Kingdom Building. It's about reflecting the heart of Christ, who reached out to the marginalized, the outcast, and the overlooked. It's about building a community that mirrors the diversity and inclusivity of God's Kingdom, where every individual is valued, loved, and welcomed. As we expand our circles, let us do so with the love and grace of Christ, knowing that in every face we encounter, we see the image of God, and in every story we hear, we witness the unfolding of His grand narrative. Let this journey be one of discovery, growth, and profound fellowship, as we embrace all those whom God brings into our lives, celebrating the beautiful diversity of His Kingdom.

Become Willing to Partner with Other Kingdom Builders Who Share the Same Commonalities

In the grand endeavor of Kingdom Building, collaboration stands as a towering pillar, essential and formidable. This chapter invites us to not only recognize but also embrace the power of partnership with fellow Kingdom Builders who share our values and visions. It's a call to join hands and hearts, merging our individual lights into a blazing torch that illuminates the path of truth and love in a world that often wanders in shadows.

Picture a group of travelers, each embarking on a journey to scale a mighty mountain. Individually, they possess unique strengths and abilities, yet the mountain before them is daunting, its peak shrouded in clouds, formidable and elusive. However, when these travelers meet, recognizing their shared goal, they decide to journey together. With each step, their individual strengths are amplified by the support and encouragement of their companions. The once-lonely journey transforms into a shared adventure, full of camaraderie, shared purpose, and a multiplied impact.

The Bible is replete with examples of such partnerships. Think of Moses and Aaron in the book of Exodus. Moses, feeling inadequate to speak before Pharaoh, was paired with Aaron by God's command. Together, they complemented each other and successfully led the Israelites out of Egypt. Their partnership demonstrates how God often pairs us with others to accomplish His greater purpose. Exodus 4:15-16 illustrates this, where God says to Moses, "You shall speak to him and put words in his mouth; I will help both of you speak and will teach you what to do."

In the New Testament, we find the apostle Paul, a fervent preacher of the gospel, often partnering with other believers. His collaborations with individuals like Barnabas, Silas, and Timothy were not just strategic but were also rooted in shared convictions and a common mission to spread the Gospel. These partnerships were instrumental in establishing the early church, showcasing the incredible impact that like-minded individuals can have when they unite for a common cause.

In today's world, the call to partner with fellow Kingdom Builders is as crucial as ever. In our communities and beyond, there are challenges too great for any one person or group to tackle alone. Be it poverty, injustice, or spiritual apathy, these are mountains that require a collective effort to scale. By partnering with those who share our values and visions, we create a synergy that can tackle larger tasks, spread the Gospel more effectively, and bring tangible change in our communities.

Such partnerships, however, require a willingness to not only share our strengths but also our vulnerabilities. It's about acknowledging that we are parts of a whole, each carrying a piece of the puzzle, and only together can we see the full picture. This concept is beautifully encapsulated in 1 Corinthians 12:12, which states, "Just as a body, though one, has many parts, but all its many parts form one body, so it is with Christ." In this scripture, we are reminded that our diversity is not a barrier but a strength, a multifaceted reflection of God's creative genius.

Collaborating with other Kingdom Builders also means embracing humility and mutual respect. It's understanding that partnership is not about dominance or superiority but about equal contribution towards a shared goal. Philippians 2:3-4 advises, "Do nothing out of selfish ambition or vain conceit. Rather, in humility value others above yourselves, not looking to your own interests but each of you to the interests of the others." This scripture guides us to approach our partnerships with a servant heart, valuing and uplifting the contributions of our fellow collaborators.

Furthermore, partnerships in Kingdom Building are not just functional arrangements; they are spiritual connections. They are relationships fostered under the guidance of the Holy Spirit, rooted in prayer and a shared commitment to follow God's will. In these partnerships, we find not only allies for our mission but also brothers and sisters in Christ, with whom we share a bond that transcends mere collaboration.

Let us be inspired to become willing partners with other Kingdom Builders. Let us seek out those who share our heart for God's work, and together, let us embark on the glorious task of advancing His Kingdom. In unity, respect, and shared vision, our efforts are not just doubled; they are multiplied, creating ripples of impact that can touch lives, transform communities, and reverberate throughout eternity. Let our partnerships be a testament to the world of the unity, love, and power found in the Body of Christ as we work hand in hand to fulfill the great commission entrusted to us.

We Have More in Common Than We Differ

In the grand pursuit of Kingdom Building, a profound truth emerges, resonating through the corridors of our collective journey – we, as followers of Christ, have more in common than we differ.

Amidst our diverse tapestry of experiences, backgrounds, and stories, lies a unifying thread, a shared purpose and set of values that bind us in Christ. This revelation isn't just a comforting thought; it's a formidable force that, when recognized and leveraged, strengthens our relationships and propels us forward in our collective mission as Kingdom Builders.

Imagine a grand mosaic, a masterpiece stretching across a vast wall. Each tile, distinct in color and shape, contributes to the overarching image. Individually, the tiles tell their own stories, unique and standalone. Yet, when seen together, they reveal a larger picture, a narrative far greater than the sum of its parts. This mosaic is akin to the Body of Christ – diverse yet united, distinct yet cohesive, different in function yet identical in importance and purpose.

The scriptural foundation for this unity is found in Galatians 3:28, "There is neither Jew nor Greek, slave nor free, nor is there male and female, for you are all one in Christ Jesus." This verse doesn't diminish our differences; rather, it elevates our common identity in Christ above all else. Our varied backgrounds, cultures, and life experiences are not barriers but enrichments, adding depth and color to the shared tapestry of our faith.

Take, for instance, the story of two believers, John and Maria. John, from a small town in the Midwest, and Maria, an immigrant from a distant country, found themselves seated next to each other in a church gathering. Their worlds seemed worlds apart – different upbringings, different cultures, and different life stories. Yet, as they engaged in conversation, they discovered a mutual love for Christ, a shared zeal for outreach, and a common passion for music. Their external differences paled in comparison to the profound commonalities in their faith and mission. This newfound friendship blossomed, showcasing the unity that Christ brings, transcending all cultural and geographical divides.

In another context, a group of believers from various denominational backgrounds came together for a community project. Initially, apprehensions loomed – would their theological differences hinder their collaboration? However, as they worked side by side, focusing on their shared vision of serving the community in Christ's love, their differences seemed trivial. They found common ground in the essentials of their faith – the lordship of Jesus, the message of the Gospel, and the call to love and serve others. This collaboration turned into a powerful testimony in the community, a living example of the unity and diversity within the Body of Christ.

This truth of our shared commonalities extends beyond personal relationships to impact our collective mission as Kingdom Builders. When we focus on what unites us – our faith in Christ, our desire to follow His teachings, and our calling to be His hands and feet in the world – we harness a powerful force for good. Together, we can tackle larger issues, address more significant needs, and make a more substantial impact than we ever could alone.

Embracing our commonalities in Christ also challenges the narrative of division and strife that often dominates our world. In a society marked by polarization and conflict, the Church stands as a beacon of unity and love. Jesus prayed for this unity in John 17:21, "that all of them may be one, Father, just as you are in me and I am in you." His prayer was not for uniformity but for a unity that reflects the relational oneness of the Trinity, a unity that bears witness to the world of the transformative power of the Gospel.

As we journey through our varied paths as Kingdom Builders, let us hold fast to the truth that we have more in common than we differ. Let us celebrate our diversity while embracing our shared identity in Christ. Let our unity in faith become our strength, our common purpose our guide, and our shared love for Christ our bond. In doing so, we embody the prayer of Jesus for His Church, shining forth as a testament to the world of the unifying, transformative power of the Gospel. Let us move forward, hand in hand, heart in heart, united in our mission, diverse in our expression, but singular in our purpose – to glorify Christ and to build His Kingdom on earth.

As we reach the conclusion of "Chapter 2: The Power of Commonalities," we find ourselves standing at the precipice of a profound realization. This chapter has taken us on a journey through the heart of what connects us as believers – a journey that reveals the immense strength inherent in our shared spiritual voyage. It's a journey that affirms our belief that our commonalities are not mere threads that bind us; they are powerful catalysts that propel us towards a unified mission, showcasing the indomitable power of collective purpose within Christ's embrace.

Throughout this chapter, we've explored the rich tapestry of relationships that are rooted in shared values, dreams, and aspirations. We've seen how these commonalities form a bridge over our external differences, creating a path of mutual understanding and respect. Like a beacon of light, they guide us through the complexities of our diverse backgrounds, illuminating the fundamental truths that unite us – our faith in Christ, our commitment to His teachings, and our shared vision for His Kingdom.

In delving into the essence of these commonalities, we've discovered that they do more than just connect us. They energize and mobilize us, collectively directing our efforts towards the grander vision of God's plan. In the synergy of our shared purpose, our individual strengths are magnified, our weaknesses compensated, and our efforts unified. This unity, fostered through our commonalities, is beautifully captured in the scriptural truth of Ecclesiastes 4:9, "Two are better than one, because they have a good return for their labor." In our togetherness, in our aligned purposes, we find greater impact and deeper fulfillment.

Our journey through this chapter has also highlighted the importance of embracing the diversity within the Body of Christ. We've learned that our differences, far from being obstacles, are opportunities to experience and express the multifaceted nature of God's Kingdom. By valuing and integrating the varied insights and perspectives of our brothers and sisters in Christ, we not only enrich our own understanding but also mirror the inclusive heart of God. In this diversity, united by our commonalities, we truly embody the image of a global, vibrant, and multifaceted Church.

As Kingdom Builders, we are reminded that our collective mission transcends individual agendas. In our united efforts, motivated by our shared love for Christ and desire to see His Kingdom come, we find a powerful expression of the Gospel. Our unity in purpose and in spirit stands as a testament to the world of the transformative power of Christ's love. John 13:35 underscores this, with Jesus saying, "By this everyone will know that you are my disciples, if you love one another." Our love, rooted in our common faith and purpose, becomes our defining witness.

In conclusion, "The Power of Commonalities" serves as a clarion call to every believer. It invites us to acknowledge, celebrate, and leverage our shared journey in Christ. It challenges us to look beyond the superficial and see the deeper connections that bind us in our quest for Kingdom Building. As we wrap up this chapter, let us carry forward the conviction that our commonalities are a source of immense strength and purpose. Let us commit to fostering relationships that are anchored in these shared truths, relationships that propel us towards a unified mission, and collectively magnify the glory of God. In embracing our commonalities, we embrace the heart of the Gospel – a message of unity, love, and purpose in Christ's encompassing embrace.

Chapter 3

Breaking Down Barriers

As we venture into Chapter 3: "Breaking Down Barriers," we embark on a vital and courageous mission within our Kingdom Building journey. This chapter serves as a clarion call, a summoning to action, beckoning us to actively dismantle the societal barriers that often hinder the unity and progress of God's people. It challenges us to rise above mere tolerance, to transcend our differences, and to forge connections that resonate with the profound inclusivity and divine love that are hallmarks of Christ's teaching.

This chapter is not just about acknowledging barriers; it's about actively engaging in the process of breaking them down. We are called to confront the walls of division – be they racial, cultural, economic, or doctrinal – that have long stood as obstacles in the Body of Christ and in the broader society. In doing so, we are heeding the Apostle Paul's exhortation in Galatians 3:28, "There is neither Jew nor Greek, slave nor free, nor is there male and female, for you are all one in Christ Jesus." This powerful statement is our banner as we seek to embody a community that reflects the unity and diversity of God's Kingdom.

In this chapter, we delve into the practical ways in which we, as Kingdom Builders, can apply the principles of the Gospel to break down barriers. We explore strategies that encourage understanding, empathy, and reconciliation. It's a journey that requires courage, humility, and persistent love – qualities exemplified by Christ in His earthly ministry.

We will also explore the stories of those who have triumphed over divisions, demonstrating the transformative power of God's love in bridging gaps and healing wounds. These narratives serve as beacons of hope and templates for our action, showing us that breaking down barriers is not only possible but imperative for the flourishing of God's Kingdom on earth.

"Breaking Down Barriers" is more than a chapter; it's a movement, a pivotal shift in how we approach our relationships and interactions within the Church and society. It's about replacing indifference with understanding, replacing division with unity, and replacing exclusion with a welcoming embrace. As we journey through these pages, let us be inspired to take up the mantle of reconciliation, to be ambassadors of Christ's love, and to actively participate in the construction of a Church and a world where barriers are replaced by bridges of grace and understanding.

Kingdom Citizens Break Down Societal Barriers by Living & Enforcing Kingdom Principles

In a world where divisions and disparities seem to be the norm, Kingdom Citizens stand as beacons of hope, called to a higher standard of living. This section of our journey in "Chapter 3: Breaking Down Barriers" is not just a call to awareness, but a mobilization for action. It's a divine mandate for Kingdom Citizens to actively break down the societal barriers that mar our landscapes, be they divisions of politics, race, gender, or social class. This chapter illuminates the strategies and insights necessary to overcome these differences, emphasizing the importance of living out and enforcing Kingdom principles as the means to transcend such divides.

Imagine a society fragmented by walls of misunderstanding and prejudice. These walls do not just separate people; they create chasms of disconnection and mistrust. Yet, amidst this fragmented landscape, Kingdom Citizens are positioned like skilled builders, equipped with the tools of God's Word and His unyielding love. Their mission? To dismantle these walls, brick by brick, through the enforcement of Kingdom principles.

The life and teachings of Jesus Christ offer the blueprint for this mission. He walked in a world riddled with its own barriers – between Jew and Samaritan, between male and female, between sinner and self-proclaimed saint. Yet, He consistently defied these societal norms. The encounter with the Samaritan woman at the well, as narrated in John 4, stands as a stark illustration. Here, Jesus not only engages with a Samaritan, breaking cultural taboos, but also speaks to a woman, further crossing gender barriers. His actions exemplify the Kingdom principle of loving inclusivity.

As Kingdom Citizens, our approach to breaking down barriers mirrors that of Christ. It begins with seeing beyond external labels and recognizing the inherent worth of every individual as a creation of God. It continues with cultivating empathy, understanding, and respectful dialogue, even in areas of disagreement. Romans 12:16 instructs us to "Live in harmony with one another; do not be proud, but be willing to associate with people of low position. Do not be conceited." This scripture is a clarion call to humility and unity, principles that are vital in bridging societal divides.

Moreover, Kingdom Citizens are tasked with being agents of reconciliation in a polarized world. This involves challenging injustices and advocating for equality and fairness, not with a spirit of divisiveness, but with a heart for healing and restoration. 2 Corinthians 5:18 reminds us that God "reconciled us to himself through Christ and gave us the ministry of reconciliation." Our role, therefore, is to mirror this reconciliation in our interactions and initiatives, fostering environments where differences are not just tolerated but celebrated.

In living out these Kingdom principles, we also confront our own prejudices and biases, allowing God's word and His Spirit to transform our perceptions and attitudes. The process of breaking down barriers begins within us – in the ways we think, speak, and act. As we align ourselves with God's principles of love, justice, and mercy, we become catalysts for change, challenging societal norms and inspiring others to join in this transformative work.

In embracing this call to action, Kingdom Citizens also find the strength in community. The task of dismantling societal barriers is not a solitary endeavor but a collective pursuit. In unity, we find the courage to confront difficult issues, the wisdom to navigate complex situations, and the support to persevere in the face of resistance.

Let us embrace our identity as Kingdom Citizens, committed to breaking down societal barriers through the enforcement and embodiment of Kingdom principles. Let us step out with boldness, armed with the love of Christ and the conviction of our calling, to build bridges of understanding and unity. In doing so, we become living testimonies of the transformative power of the Gospel, demonstrating to the world that in Christ, there is neither Jew nor Greek, slave nor free, male nor female, but all are one (Galatians 3:28). Our commitment to breaking down barriers is not just an act of social responsibility; it is an act of obedience to our King, a manifestation of His Kingdom on earth.

Stand Firm on Kingdom Principles

In the noble and challenging mission of breaking down societal barriers, one foundational truth remains unshakable: the necessity of standing firm on Kingdom principles. This unwavering stance is not just a choice but a mandate for every believer who seeks to navigate the tumultuous waters of societal divisions and disparities. The principles of love, peace, justice, and unity, central to the teachings of Christ, form the bedrock upon which our actions and interactions must be based. They are the compass that guides us through the storm, the anchor that holds us steady, and the light that illuminates our path in a world often clouded by conflict and misunderstanding.

Picture a vast, stormy ocean, with waves of discord and division threatening to overwhelm and capsize the boats of those who traverse its waters. In this tumultuous scene, the boat of the Kingdom Citizen, though buffeted by the same tumultuous waves, navigates with a sense of purpose and direction. This steadiness doesn't come from the skill of the sailor alone but from the unerring compass of Kingdom principles that guide the boat. The principles of love, peace, justice, and unity are like the four cardinal points on this compass, directing every decision, every action, and every response.

Consider the principle of love, as epitomized in 1 Corinthians 13:4-7. Love, in its purest Kingdom form, is patient, kind, and devoid of envy or boastfulness. It is not proud, dishonoring, or self-seeking. In a society where division often stems from pride, envy, and selfish ambitions, standing firm in love becomes a radical act, a counter-cultural stance that breaks down barriers and fosters understanding and compassion.

Peace, another cornerstone of Kingdom living, is beautifully described in Matthew 5:9, "Blessed are the peacemakers, for they will be called children of God." To stand firm on this principle is to actively seek reconciliation, to be a bridge-builder in a world rife with walls of separation. It involves creating spaces of dialogue and understanding, even in the midst of conflict and disagreement.

Justice, too, is a non-negotiable Kingdom principle. Micah 6:8 succinctly captures this call, "And what does the LORD require of you? To act justly and to love mercy and to walk humbly with your God." Standing firm in justice means advocating for the marginalized, the oppressed, and the voiceless. It means challenging systems and structures that perpetuate inequality and standing in solidarity with those who suffer injustice.

Finally, unity, as exemplified in Jesus' prayer in John 17:21 – "that all of them may be one, Father, just as you are in me and I am in you" – is the ultimate goal of our efforts to break down barriers. To stand firm on this principle is to strive for a community where diversity is celebrated, differences are respected, and the bond of shared faith in Christ overrides all else.

Living out these principles in the face of societal divisions is not an easy task. It requires courage, commitment, and a willingness to sometimes stand against the tide. It involves difficult conversations, challenging confrontations, and unwavering adherence to what we know to be true in God's Word.

Yet, in this adherence, there is immense power. When we stand firm on Kingdom principles, we become conduits of God's grace, agents of His transformative work in the world. We become lights in the darkness, salt in a world that often tastes bland with conformity and injustice. Our steadfastness becomes a testimony, a beacon that draws others to the truth and love of Christ.

As Kingdom Citizens, our call to break down barriers is deeply intertwined with our commitment to live out these unshakable principles. Each act of love, each effort to make peace, each stand for justice, and each endeavor to promote unity is a step towards fulfilling God's vision for His Church and His world.

Let us be encouraged to stand firm on these principles. Let us be emboldened to view and engage with the world through the lens of love, peace, justice, and unity. In the face of societal divisions, let these principles guide our actions and interactions. Let us remember that our unwavering adherence to these truths not only upholds God's standards but also fosters a spirit of reconciliation and understanding. In standing firm on Kingdom principles, we do more than just navigate societal challenges; we actively participate in the manifestation of God's Kingdom on earth, reflecting His heart and His ways in a world that desperately needs His touch.

Understand that Warfare is Part of Breaking Down Barriers

In the journey of breaking down societal barriers, we navigate a path that is not merely challenging; it is fraught with spiritual warfare. This section of our odyssey through "Chapter 3: Breaking Down Barriers" brings us to the stark realization that the endeavor to dismantle walls of division is a battle not against flesh and blood, but against forces and principalities that seek to disrupt and divide the Body of Christ. As Kingdom Citizens, our understanding of this reality is crucial, equipping us to engage these challenges not with the weapons of the world but with the armor of God – prayer, faith, and His unerring Word. It is on this spiritual battleground that the formidable walls of division crumble and true unity is forged.

Imagine a vast field where two kingdoms stand at odds. The Kingdom of Light, under the banner of Christ, is called to advance into territories held by the Kingdom of Darkness. The battle is not for land or riches but for the hearts and minds of people, for the unity and integrity of the Church. Ephesians 6:12 reminds us, "For our struggle is not against flesh and blood, but against the rulers, against the authorities, against the powers of this dark world and against the spiritual forces of evil in the heavenly realms." In this verse lies the key to our strategy – our battle is spiritual, and so are our weapons.

Consider the story of Nehemiah, tasked with rebuilding the walls of Jerusalem. His mission was not just a physical reconstruction but also a spiritual revival. He faced opposition, ridicule, and threats from those who wished to see the walls remain in ruin. Nehemiah's response to these challenges was not one of violence or aggression but of prayer and faith. In Nehemiah 4:20, he declares, "Our God will fight for us." His trust in God's protection and guidance was his greatest weapon, and it was through this spiritual fortitude that the walls of Jerusalem were rebuilt.

In our present day, the battle to break down barriers of race, gender, class, and cultural differences mirrors Nehemiah's challenge. We confront ideologies and systems that perpetuate division and inequality. These barriers, deeply ingrained in societies and even within the Church, require more than human effort to dismantle; they require divine intervention.

This is where our spiritual arsenal comes into play. Prayer becomes our first line of defense and our constant source of strength. In prayer, we seek God's guidance, wisdom, and strength to face the challenges ahead. We follow the directive of 2 Chronicles 7:14, "If my people, who are called by my name, will humble themselves and pray and seek my face and turn from their wicked ways, then I will hear from heaven, and I will forgive their sin and will heal their land." In this verse, we find the promise of divine intervention when we approach God with humility and reliance.

Faith, too, is a critical weapon in our arsenal. In the face of seemingly insurmountable barriers, faith gives us the conviction that "with God all things are possible" (Matthew 19:26). It's faith that empowers us to believe in the possibility of change, in the healing of divisions, and in the unity of the Body of Christ.

The Word of God is our sword, cutting through lies, misconceptions, and prejudices. It is through the truth of God's Word that we challenge the ideologies that divide us. Scriptures like Galatians 3:28, "There is neither Jew nor Greek, there is neither slave nor free, there is no male and female, for you are all one in Christ Jesus," become rallying cries in our mission to break down barriers.

In this spiritual warfare, our approach is not one of aggression but of love, peace, and reconciliation. We are called to mirror the character of Christ, who broke down the ultimate barrier – the separation between God and man – through His sacrificial love. It's in embodying this Christ-like love and humility that we become effective agents of change, tearing down walls of division and building bridges of unity.

Let us be galvanized to understand that warfare is indeed a part of breaking down barriers. Armed with prayer, fortified by faith, and guided by the Word of God, we advance into this battle, not in fear or despair, but with the assurance of victory in Christ. Let us stand firm, united in our resolve to see the walls of division fall and the banner of Christ's love and unity be lifted high. In this spiritual battle, we are not only contenders; we are more than conquerors through Him who loved us (Romans 8:37). Let our efforts to dismantle societal barriers be a testament to the world of the transformative, unifying power of the Gospel.

Be Strategic

In the ongoing quest to dismantle the barriers that fragment our society and hinder the full expression of God's Kingdom, being strategic is not merely a suggestion; it is a necessity. This section propels us into the realm of thoughtful planning and discerning action. As Kingdom Builders, we are called to approach the challenge of barrier-breaking not haphazardly, but with precision and intentionality, crafting targeted approaches that speak directly to the heart of the issues we face.

Imagine a group of architects planning to build a bridge over a tumultuous river. The task is not merely about connecting two landmasses; it's about understanding the currents, the geography, and the needs of those who will cross this bridge. Similarly, in our mission to bridge societal divides, we must be like these architects – keenly aware of the specific challenges and obstacles within our contexts, and armed with well-thought-out strategies to address them.

Our strategic approach begins with a clear understanding of the barriers we seek to dismantle. Like the sons of Issachar, who "understood the times and knew what Israel should do" (1 Chronicles 12:32), we need discernment to identify the underlying issues that feed division and strife within our communities. This discernment is more than intellectual awareness; it's a spiritual sensitivity, honed through prayer and guided by the Holy Spirit.

One effective strategy in this endeavor is intentional cross-cultural engagement. This means stepping out of our cultural comfort zones to build relationships with those who come from different backgrounds. It involves not just passive interaction but active involvement and immersion into the lives and experiences of others. Like the Apostle Paul, who became "all things to all people" (1 Corinthians 9:22), we too must be adaptable and empathetic in our approach, seeking common ground while respecting and celebrating our differences.

Education and awareness campaigns are also vital tools in our strategic arsenal. Often, barriers are fortified by ignorance and misconceptions. By providing platforms for education – be it through workshops, seminars, discussions, or even informal gatherings – we can dispel myths, broaden perspectives, and cultivate a more informed and empathetic community. These campaigns should not only focus on the issues but also highlight the biblical principles of love, justice, and unity that underpin our quest for barrier-breaking.

Moreover, advocating for equitable practices is an essential part of our strategy. In a world where systemic inequalities often underlie societal divisions, our call is to be voices for justice and fairness. This might involve challenging unjust policies, supporting initiatives that promote equality, or simply standing in solidarity with those who are marginalized. In doing so, we live out the call of Micah 6:8, "to act justly and to love mercy and to walk humbly with your God."

Being strategic also means being proactive in creating spaces and opportunities for inclusive community building. It's about orchestrating environments – whether in our churches, workplaces, or neighborhoods – where diversity is not just tolerated but embraced and celebrated. It's about fostering dialogues that bridge gaps, initiatives that bring people together, and activities that highlight our shared humanity.

In our pursuit of breaking down barriers, our strategies must be coupled with patience and perseverance. The walls of division did not arise overnight, and they will not fall in a day. Our efforts require a long-term commitment, a resilience to continue even when progress seems slow, and faith to believe that with God, all things are possible.

Let us be inspired to approach the task of breaking down barriers with strategic minds and prayerful hearts. Let our actions be deliberate, our plans well-crafted, and our efforts sustained. In being strategic, we are not just participants in the mission of God's Kingdom; we are co-laborers with Christ, working diligently and thoughtfully to see His will done on earth as it is in heaven. Let us move forward with the wisdom of serpents and the innocence of doves (Matthew 10:16), strategically advancing the cause of Christ and embodying the unity, love, and peace He so passionately desires for His Church.

Remain Faithful to God and Your Team

In breaking down societal barriers, two virtues emerge as indispensable – faithfulness to God and unwavering commitment to our team. As Kingdom Builders, our journey is marked not only by the goals we seek to achieve but by the steadfastness of our walk with God and the unity within our ranks. This section of our narrative illuminates the essentiality of these virtues, painting a picture of a mission that thrives on divine alignment and communal strength.

Envision a band of climbers, each tethered to one another, ascending a formidable mountain. Their goal is lofty, their path fraught with challenges. Yet, what binds them is more than ropes – it's a shared commitment to reach the summit together. In this image, we find a reflection of our journey in breaking down barriers. Just as climbers rely on mutual support and shared focus, we, as Kingdom Builders, rely on our faithfulness to God's calling and our solidarity as a team.

Faithfulness to God is the compass that guides our path. It's the commitment to seek His will in every decision, to align our actions with His purposes, and to trust in His timing and plan. Like the Psalmist declares in Psalm 37:5, "Commit your way to the Lord; trust in him, and he will act." This scripture is a reminder that our efforts, when rooted in a deep trust and commitment to God, bear fruit beyond our capabilities. Our journey in dismantling societal barriers is undergirded by this commitment to stay true to God's calling, to lean not on our understanding but to acknowledge Him in all our ways (Proverbs 3:5-6).

Consider the story of Nehemiah, a cupbearer who became a wall builder. His mission to rebuild the walls of Jerusalem was steeped in faithfulness to God. He sought God's guidance in prayer, heeded His instructions, and remained steadfast amidst opposition. Nehemiah's unwavering commitment to God ensured that his efforts were aligned with divine purposes, turning what seemed like an insurmountable task into a triumphant victory for God's people.

Equally crucial in our mission is the commitment to our team. The journey of breaking down barriers is not a solitary endeavor but a collective effort. Maintaining unity and support within our team is vital for success. It provides the strength and encouragement needed, especially when progress seems slow or opposition looms large. The Apostle Paul, in Ephesians 4:3, urges us to "make every effort to keep the unity of the Spirit through the bond of peace." This unity is not merely about agreeing on everything; it's about respecting each other's perspectives, supporting one another in challenges, and celebrating each other's successes.

The unity and strength of a team are beautifully depicted in the account of Aaron and Hur supporting Moses' hands during the battle against the Amalekites in Exodus 17. As long as Moses' hands were raised, Israel prevailed, but when he grew tired, Aaron and Hur held his hands up. This picture of support and unity exemplifies the power of a committed team – together, they achieved what would have been impossible alone.

In our teams, each member brings unique gifts, perspectives, and skills. These differences, far from being a source of division, are a source of strength. In Romans 12:4-5, we are reminded, "For just as each of us has one body with many members, and these members do not all have the same function, so in Christ we, though many, form one body, and each member belongs to all the others." Our commitment to each other is a reflection of our commitment to Christ, a manifestation of the unity He desires for His body.

Remaining faithful to God and committed to our team also means navigating conflicts and misunderstandings with grace and understanding. It's about having difficult conversations in love, bearing with one another in compassion, and forgiving as Christ forgave us (Colossians 3:13). In doing so, we not only maintain the integrity of our team but also exemplify the character of Christ to a watching world.

Let us embrace the call to remain faithful to God and steadfast in our commitment to our team. Let our efforts in breaking down barriers be steeped in a deep trust in God and a resilient unity with our fellow Kingdom Builders. Let us remember that in our faithfulness and unity, we find the strength, courage, and perseverance needed to overcome obstacles and bring forth the change we seek. In standing together, anchored in God's will and bound by mutual support, we become more than a team; we become a force of transformation, reflecting God's love and unity in a divided world.

Remember The Goal

In the heart of the arduous yet noble undertaking of dismantling societal barriers lies a beacon that must never dim – the goal of advancing the Kingdom of God. This chapter, etched with the challenges and triumphs of breaking barriers, continually points us back to this central tenet. It's a journey that transcends mere social reform, embedding us deeply into the fabric of a far grander narrative – the establishment of God's reign of peace, justice, and love in every corner of society. Keeping this goal at the forefront ensures that our efforts, steeped in sweat and sometimes tears, are not in vain but contribute profoundly to an eternal purpose.

Imagine a grand mural depicting a myriad of people, from every nation and walk of life, working together to construct a magnificent edifice. Each person plays a crucial role, whether laying bricks, offering water, or drawing plans. Amidst the bustle, there's a noticeable unity and singleness of purpose. This mural is a depiction of our task in breaking down societal barriers – a collective effort where each action, no matter how small, contributes to the completion of the divine masterpiece.

The Apostle Paul, in his letter to the Corinthians, reminds us of this singleness of purpose. In 1 Corinthians 10:31, he writes, "So whether you eat or drink or whatever you do, do it all for the glory of God." Here, Paul is not merely addressing religious activities; he is speaking of every facet of our lives. Our efforts to break down societal barriers are not just social or political acts; they are spiritual acts that reflect the glory of God and His kingdom values.

Consider the story of Queen Esther. Placed in a position of influence, she could have easily enjoyed the comforts of her palace life. Yet, she understood that her role was part of a bigger plan – the salvation of her people. When Mordecai reminded her that she was positioned "for such a time as this" (Esther 4:14), it was a call to remember her goal. Esther's subsequent actions, marked by courage and wisdom, were not just for the immediate rescue of her people but were instrumental in preserving the lineage through which the Savior of the world would come.

In our communities, the task of breaking down barriers of race, class, gender, and culture is part of our contribution to this grand design. It's about creating spaces where the values of God's

Kingdom – love, justice, peace, and reconciliation – are not just ideals but living realities. Our actions, whether advocating for the marginalized, fostering cross-cultural dialogues, or challenging unjust systems, are threads woven into the tapestry of God's Kingdom.

In this endeavor, it's crucial to anchor our efforts in prayer and scripture. The Psalms often remind us of the importance of aligning our actions with God's will. Psalm 127:1 says, "Unless the Lord builds the house, the builders labor in vain." Our efforts to break down barriers must be bathed in prayer, seeking God's guidance and wisdom, ensuring that our labor is in sync with His divine blueprint.

Furthermore, our goal to advance God's Kingdom calls us to a higher standard of action. It's not just about what we do, but how we do it. Our methods must reflect the character of Christ – marked by love, grace, and humility. The Sermon on the Mount, particularly the Beatitudes (Matthew 5:1-12), lays out the attitudes and behaviors befitting those who are building God's Kingdom.

As we journey in breaking down barriers, it's also important to celebrate the small victories along the way. Each barrier broken, each bridge built, is a step closer to realizing the fullness of God's Kingdom on earth. These milestones should serve as reminders of God's faithfulness and the power of collective action aligned with divine purpose.

As we strive to dismantle the walls that divide, let us continually remember our ultimate goal – the advancement of God's Kingdom. This goal transcends our earthly objectives, infusing our efforts with eternal significance. Let our actions, anchored in the principles of God's Word and fueled by His Spirit, contribute not just to temporary reforms but to the everlasting impact of His Kingdom. Let us move forward with the conviction that our labor in the Lord is not in vain (1 Corinthians 15:58), contributing to a legacy that will outlast our time on earth and resonate throughout eternity. In remembering our goal, we find the strength, purpose, and perseverance to continue this noble endeavor, building a future where God's love, justice, and peace reign supreme.

God Has Given Us Power & Authority to Break Down Barriers That Would Hinder The Kingdom of God

In the divinely appointed mission to transform society and advance the Kingdom of God, we, as Kingdom Citizens, are neither bystanders nor powerless spectators. God, in His infinite wisdom and grace, has endowed us with power and authority – not as the world gives, but as only the Sovereign Lord can. This power and authority are our divine endowment to break down the barriers that hinder His Kingdom, to stand as agents of change in a world rife with divisions, and to build bridges where walls of separation have long stood. This part of our narrative is not about mere societal transformation; it's about manifesting the reality of God's Kingdom on earth.

Imagine a medieval city surrounded by high walls, impenetrable and daunting. Within these walls, life is segmented and disjointed, communities isolated by barriers both visible and invisible. Now envision a group of determined builders, each equipped with tools not of iron and steel, but of divine origin. These builders are

Kingdom Citizens, and their mission is to dismantle these walls, stone by stone. Luke 10:19 says, "I have given you authority to trample on snakes and scorpions and to overcome all the power of the enemy; nothing will harm you." Herein lies the essence of our authority – an empowerment to overcome the forces that divide and to establish God's reign of peace and unity.

Consider the story of Joshua leading the Israelites to conquer Jericho. Faced with the daunting walls of the city, Joshua didn't rely on conventional warfare tactics. Instead, he followed God's instruction, marching around the city and blowing trumpets, a seemingly irrational strategy by human standards. Yet, in this act of obedience and faith, the walls of Jericho fell, paving the way for Israel's victory. This historical moment (Joshua 6) is a testament to the power and authority we hold when we align ourselves with God's will and purposes.

In our times, the barriers may be different – racial injustice, economic disparity, cultural misunderstandings, religious intolerance – but the principle remains the same. We are called to be like Joshua, marching not with physical weapons but armed with faith, prayer, the Word of God, and the love of Christ. These are the tools with which we dismantle barriers, tools that are mighty in God for pulling down strongholds (2 Corinthians 10:4).

Our role as agents of change requires more than passive acknowledgment of this authority; it calls for active engagement. It's about identifying areas where societal divisions are most prevalent and using our God-given authority to bring healing and reconciliation. Whether it's through advocating for justice, engaging in peacemaking initiatives, or simply extending Christ's love in our everyday interactions, we are called to be the embodiment of God's transformative power.

Furthermore, breaking down these barriers is a communal effort, a reflection of the collective power within the Body of Christ. Just as the early church in Acts 2:44-47 shared everything and lived in unity, we too are called to unite in this mission. Our combined efforts, rooted in our shared faith and empowered by the Holy Spirit, become a formidable force against the divisions that plague our societies.

Our approach in this endeavor is marked by Christ's example – an approach of humility, service, and sacrificial love. Jesus, in washing His disciples' feet, demonstrated the leadership and authority we are called to emulate (John 13:3-17). It's an authority exercised not in domination or coercion, but in service and love – breaking down the greatest barrier of all, the barrier of sin and separation from God.

As Kingdom Citizens, we must also be discerning, understanding that not every societal norm aligns with God's Kingdom principles. Our challenge is to distinguish between traditions and norms that foster community and those that create division. This discernment requires constant communion with God, seeking His guidance and wisdom in every step (James 1:5).

As we embrace our calling to break down barriers, let us do so with the confidence that God has equipped us with the necessary power and authority. Let our actions reflect the heart of God, our strategies be guided by His wisdom, and our efforts be fueled by His love. In breaking down these barriers, we are not merely engaging in social reform; we are actively participating in the unfolding of God's Kingdom on earth. Let us march forward with faith and determination, knowing that in God, we have the victory, and through Him, we can accomplish far more than we can ask or imagine (Ephesians 3:20).

We are empowered with a vision of a united world, where barriers are replaced with bridges of understanding, showcasing the transformative and inclusive power of God's Kingdom.

As we draw the curtains on "Chapter 3: Breaking Down Barriers," we stand at the precipice of a profound realization – we are not just agents of change; we are harbingers of a vision. This vision is grand and glorious, painting a picture of a world transformed, where the walls that divide us crumble under the weight of God's unyielding love, and in their place rise bridges of understanding and connection. It's a vision of a united world, transcending societal, cultural, and racial divides, showcasing the transformative and inclusive power of God's Kingdom.

This chapter has taken us on a journey, not just through the theories and strategies of breaking down barriers, but through the very heart of what it means to live as Kingdom Citizens. We have been reminded that in Christ, there is no Jew or Gentile, no slave or free, no male or female – for we are all one in Him (Galatians 3:28). This unity is not a mere idealistic dream; it's a divine mandate, a calling that we, as bearers of His image and followers of His teachings, are empowered to bring into fruition.

The vision we carry is one of reconciliation and peace, echoing the reconciliation that Christ accomplished on the cross. It's a vision where love triumphs over hatred, where grace overcomes judgment, and where understanding dispels ignorance. In this vision, the barriers of prejudice, misunderstanding, and fear are dismantled, not by human might or wisdom, but by the transformative power of the Gospel.

As Kingdom Citizens, we recognize that this vision is not realized through passive waiting or wishful thinking. It demands action, courage, and perseverance. It calls us to be active participants in the ministry of reconciliation, to be ambassadors of Christ's love in a broken and divided world. Our role is to mirror the inclusivity and love of our Savior, extending His grace to the marginalized, His understanding to the misunderstood, and His peace to the conflicted.

The path to this united world is paved with challenges, but it is also lined with hope – the hope found in the promises of God, the hope bolstered by the victories of the past, and the hope that shines bright in the actions of those committed to this cause. As we close this chapter, let us embrace this vision with renewed zeal and commitment. Let us stride forward, armed with the knowledge that we are not alone in this endeavor – we are backed by the power of the Holy Spirit, guided by the wisdom of God's Word, and united with fellow believers across the globe.

In our pursuit to replace barriers with bridges, let us hold fast to the truth that our efforts are part of a greater plan – the establishment of God's Kingdom on earth as it is in heaven. Let this vision inspire us, guide us, and drive us forward. Let us work tirelessly, knowing that each step we take towards breaking down barriers is a step closer to realizing the unity and harmony that God desires for His creation. Let us go forth with the assurance that in God, we have the strength, the resources, and the resolve to transform this vision into reality, showcasing the boundless, inclusive love of God's Kingdom to a world in need.

Chapter 4

Embracing Diversity

As we turn the pages to Chapter 4, "Embracing Diversity," we enter a realm that celebrates the multifaceted beauty of God's creation. In this chapter, we are invited to explore and revel in the strength and splendor that diversity brings to our Kingdom community. It's a call to view our differences not as barriers, but as divine gifts – vibrant threads woven into the rich tapestry of our faith journey. This chapter is an exhortation to embrace and integrate the varied hues of humanity into the colorful mosaic that is the Body of Christ.

In a world often fragmented by lines of division, this chapter serves as a reminder of the profound unity found in our diversity. The scriptural call in 1 Corinthians 12:12-14, "For just as the body is one and has many members, and all the members of the body, though many, are one body, so it is with Christ," underpins our exploration. Here, the Apostle Paul paints a picture of the church as a body – diverse yet unified, distinct yet indispensable. This imagery challenges us to recognize the value and necessity of each individual's unique contribution to the Kingdom of God.

This chapter takes us on a journey to discover how our individual backgrounds, experiences, cultures, and perspectives are not just mere variations but essential components of God's Kingdom. We will explore how embracing this diversity enriches our understanding of God, enhances our worship, and deepens our fellowship. It's about celebrating the diversity in our churches, communities, and individual lives as reflections of God's infinite creativity and love.

Furthermore, "Embracing Diversity" is more than an acknowledgment – it's an active process of inclusion. It involves breaking down preconceived notions, opening our hearts to learn from each other, and actively seeking to understand perspectives different from our own. It's a journey marked by listening, learning, and loving in a way that reflects the heart of Jesus Christ, who crossed cultural and societal boundaries to demonstrate God's love for all humanity.

As we delve into this chapter, let us be inspired to not just tolerate but truly celebrate our differences. Let us cultivate a Kingdom culture where every individual, irrespective of their background, is valued, heard, and appreciated. Let us embrace the diverse expressions of faith and worship, knowing that each one brings a unique flavor to our collective experience of God.

In embracing diversity, we are not just enriching our own faith journey; we are actively participating in the manifestation of God's Kingdom on earth – a kingdom characterized by its diversity and unified in its purpose. As we navigate through this chapter, let our hearts be open to the beautiful possibilities that diversity holds, and let our communities be transformed into vibrant reflections of God's inclusive and boundless love.

Diversity is the Spice of Life

In the intricate and colorful mosaic of human existence, diversity represents the myriad hues that bring depth, beauty, and resilience to the fabric of our communities and individual lives. "Diversity is the Spice of Life," this chapter's vibrant refrain, celebrates the richness of diversity, unfolding how its embrace enriches and invigorates our collective journey as Kingdom Citizens. It is a spirited call to recognize and relish the multitude of ways our differences enhance our communal tapestry, fostering a profound understanding of God's diverse creation.

Picture a flourishing garden, where each plant, flower, and tree contributes its unique character to the garden's splendor. The diversity within this garden — the variety in colors, textures, and fragrances — is what makes it captivating and complete. Just like this garden, our world is a beautiful blend of cultures, ethnicities, ideas, and experiences, each adding its distinct flavor to the human experience.

The divine design behind this diversity is highlighted in Genesis 1:27, "So God created mankind in his own image, in the image of God he created them; male and female he created them." This verse not only affirms the inherent worth and dignity of every person but also reveals the Creator's intent in fashioning such diversity.

Humanity, in all its varied forms, mirrors the multifaceted nature of God Himself.

This chapter takes us on a voyage of understanding how embracing diversity contributes to the vitality and resilience of our communities. It's about evolving from mere tolerance to a deep-seated appreciation and celebration of our differences. Diversity introduces a wealth of perspectives and experiences that strengthen and enrich our communities, igniting creativity, promoting empathy, and widening our worldview.

Embracing diversity requires an active effort — challenging our biases, stepping out of our comfort zones, and engaging with those who differ from us. It's a journey of listening and learning, opening ourselves to the stories and life experiences of others, much like Jesus did in His life, reaching across cultural and societal boundaries with love and compassion.

We explore narratives of individuals and communities profoundly transformed by the richness of diversity. Stories from churches, organizations, and groups illustrate how embracing diverse memberships enhances effectiveness and impact, reinforcing the notion that diversity can deepen our capacity to connect and serve each other.

Furthermore, this chapter underscores diversity's role in offering a richer understanding of God's creation. Much like an artist uses a range of colors to create a beautiful painting, God employs the diversity of humanity to paint the canvas of life. Recognizing and valuing this diversity allows us to appreciate the Creator's artistry more fully.

Let us be inspired to view diversity as the spice that enlivens our existence. Let's commit to embracing and celebrating our differences, recognizing them as gifts that enrich our shared experience. In striving to create communities where diversity is not only accepted but honored, we not only forge a more robust, empathetic Kingdom community but also reflect the inclusivity and love inherent in the Kingdom of God. May our celebration of diversity be a testament to the world of the beauty and strength found in unity amidst diversity, a preview of heaven on earth, united under our shared faith in Christ.

Visit Local Community Groups

In the enriching journey of embracing diversity, one of the most practical and profound steps we can take is to step outside the familiar boundaries of our daily lives and venture into the world of local community groups. These groups, often a vibrant microcosm of broader society, offer a kaleidoscope of cultures, backgrounds, and perspectives. Engaging with these communities is an adventure that calls us to leave our comfort zones, challenge our preconceptions, and forge connections with people we might not otherwise encounter. This engagement is more than just a passive observation; it's an active immersion, a heartfelt participation in the life and rhythm of these diverse communities.

Imagine yourself as a traveler, stepping into a new city where every street corner, every market, and every gathering place buzzes with the stories and lives of its people. This is what visiting local community groups feels like – a journey into the heart of diversity, an opportunity to experience firsthand the rich tapestry of humanity in all its myriad forms.

In these community groups, every interaction, every conversation is an opportunity to learn and grow. It's in these settings that barriers of misunderstanding and stereotypes are often dismantled. As we listen to stories, share meals, and participate in activities, our worldview expands, and our appreciation for diversity deepens.

The Bible encourages such engagement with our communities. In Hebrews 13:2, we are reminded, "Do not forget to show hospitality to strangers, for by so doing some people have shown hospitality to angels without knowing it." This scripture speaks to the heart of engaging with local community groups – it's an exercise in hospitality, openness, and learning from others.

One might consider the story of the early church in Acts, where believers from various backgrounds came together, breaking bread in their homes, and sharing their lives with each other (Acts 2:46-47). This communal way of living was not just about fellowship; it was a powerful expression of the diverse yet united body of Christ. In visiting local community groups, we mirror this early church's spirit, building bridges across cultural and social divides.

Participating in these local groups often leads to unexpected discoveries about others and ourselves. We might find common ground with people from seemingly different worlds, or we might be challenged to re-evaluate long-held beliefs. Through this, we embody the teaching of Philippians 2:4 – "not looking to your own interests but each of you to the interests of the others." In stepping into the lives of others, we practice empathy, solidarity, and love.

Furthermore, our engagement with community groups is not a one-way street; it's a mutual exchange. We not only learn from these communities, but we also have the opportunity to contribute – to share our own stories, skills, and perspectives. It's in this give-and-take that true community is forged – a community where differences are not just tolerated but celebrated.

Engaging with local community groups can take many forms – from participating in cultural festivals, attending community meetings, volunteering in local projects, or even joining a class or workshop. Each of these activities provides a window into the lives of others and offers a chance to build meaningful relationships.

Let's be inspired to take the step of visiting local community groups as a tangible act of embracing diversity. Let's approach these experiences with open hearts and minds, ready to learn, share, and grow. In doing so, we are not just expanding our personal horizons; we are actively participating in the building of a more inclusive, empathetic, and diverse Kingdom community. Let our foray into these local groups be marked by the love and grace of Christ, reflecting His heart for all people. And as we weave in and out of the beautiful mosaic of these communities, may we find joy in the journey and hope in the connections we make, knowing that each step we take is a step toward a more united and understanding world.

Be Open to Fellowship with Others In and Outside Your Religion

Embarking on the journey of embracing diversity calls us to expand our boundaries, stepping beyond the familiar borders of our own religious traditions to engage in fellowship with individuals from a spectrum of belief systems. This proactive pursuit of open and meaningful connections enriches our understanding of faith, spirituality, and the broader world. It's in this rich tapestry of varied experiences and beliefs where we uncover the shared threads of humanity, cultivating a ground fertile with mutual respect and understanding.

Consider the world as a grand, diverse garden where each plant, with its unique form and fragrance, contributes to the garden's overall beauty and health. In the same way, the varied beliefs and cultures of our world add distinct flavors and textures to the human experience. By engaging with those from different religious backgrounds, we add our own unique qualities to this garden, enriching its diversity and vibrancy.

The Bible itself encourages such open-minded engagement. In Acts 17:22-23, the Apostle Paul, amidst the philosophers of Athens, chooses not to confront but to connect, finding common ground in their mutual search for truth. Paul's respectful and curious approach in Athens serves as a model for us: engage with those of different faiths not in confrontation, but with a desire to understand and connect.

This journey of fellowship goes beyond mere conversation. It's an active engagement with the hearts and minds of others, through shared experiences, meaningful dialogue, and collaborative endeavors. These interactions allow us to glean insights from various worldviews, appreciate others' values and beliefs, and enrich our own understanding of faith.

Such fellowship also dispels misconceptions and stereotypes, fostering dialogues where misunderstandings are clarified, and similarities are discovered. These interactions counteract the divisions often caused by religious differences, showcasing the potential for unity and mutual respect.

Moreover, this approach mirrors Jesus' own interactions. His engagements with Samaritans, tax collectors, and gentiles broke societal norms and exemplified radical inclusivity. By following His example of extending grace and love beyond traditional boundaries, we embody the essence of His teachings.

Interacting with diverse religious backgrounds can reinforce our faith, teaching us to hold our beliefs with humility and openness. This humility is a strength, reflecting spiritual maturity and wisdom.

By fostering relationships across different religions, we mirror the broad, inclusive vision of God's Kingdom. We reflect the heart of God, who loves the entire world (John 3:16), beyond cultural and religious divisions. Our belief in a God who transcends boundaries is thus expressed in our actions and interactions.

Let's be inspired to engage in fellowship with people of various religions. Let's approach these relationships with Christ-like love, grace, and humility. Our interactions can build bridges of understanding, create channels of mutual respect, and showcase the inclusivity of God's Kingdom. By embracing this diversity, we enrich our spiritual journey and contribute to a world where differences are celebrated, commonalities embraced, and the shared fabric of humanity is respected and cherished. Let our fellowship be a beacon of hope, showcasing the unifying power of love in a diverse world.

Join a Prayer Group

In deepening our faith and embracing diversity, joining a prayer group that celebrates a spectrum of traditions and expressions can be a transformative adventure. It's a venture that takes us beyond the boundaries of our personal spiritual practices into a world where diverse streams of faith converge, enriching and strengthening our own connection with God. In these groups, a beautiful symphony of prayers rises, each voice distinct yet harmoniously interwoven, creating an atmosphere where the Spirit moves powerfully, drawing us closer to the heart of God and to each other.

Picture a gathering where believers from various backgrounds come together, united by a common desire to seek God's face. In this gathering, prayers are lifted in multiple languages, each carrying the unique inflections and rhythms of its cultural heritage. Some pray kneeling, others standing; some with lifted hands, others with bowed heads. The diversity in prayer styles and expressions is not a source of division but a cause for celebration. It is a vivid illustration of the Apostle Paul's words in 1 Corinthians 12:12-14, where he describes the church as one body with many parts, each distinct but indispensable to the whole.

Within such a prayer group, stories and testimonies are shared, weaving a rich narrative of God's work across different lives and circumstances. There's an opportunity to learn from one another's spiritual journeys, to draw wisdom from various traditions, and to see the multifaceted ways in which God interacts with His people. This learning is not merely intellectual; it is deeply spiritual, as it expands our understanding of prayer and enriches our relationship with God.

Imagine, for instance, being part of a prayer group where an elderly woman, rooted in traditional liturgical practices, prays with a sense of reverence and awe that speaks of a lifetime of walking with God. Beside her, a young man from a charismatic background prays with passionate and spontaneous expressions of faith. In another corner, a couple who have spent years in missionary work in different parts of the world share prayers infused with global perspectives and intercessory zeal for nations. In this beautiful mosaic of prayer, each participant not only contributes their unique voice but also learns from the others, creating a tapestry of faith expressions that beautifully represents the diversity within the Body of Christ.

Engaging in such a diverse prayer group aligns with Jesus' teaching on prayer in the Sermon on the Mount (Matthew 6:5-13). He emphasized sincerity in prayer, intimacy with the Father, and the seeking of His Kingdom – principles that transcend cultural and denominational lines. In these prayer groups, as we uphold these principles, our focus shifts from our differences to our shared pursuit of God's presence and will.

Moreover, these prayer groups often become a place of support and fellowship. Galatians 6:2 encourages us to "bear one another's burdens, and so fulfill the law of Christ." As group members share their struggles and triumphs, the prayer group becomes a source of encouragement and a place where burdens are lifted in communal prayer. The joys and challenges of each member are shared by all, fostering a sense of family and community that is grounded in Christ's love.

Joining a diverse prayer group also broadens our perspective on God's Kingdom. It's a reminder that the body of Christ is global and varied, yet united in its devotion to God. In these groups, we learn to appreciate and respect traditions and practices that are different from our own, which in turn fosters a spirit of unity and mutual respect within the larger church community.

Let us be encouraged to seek out and join diverse prayer groups. Let us embrace the opportunity to experience the richness of faith expressions within the Body of Christ. In doing so, we not only deepen our own spiritual lives but also contribute to building a vibrant, inclusive, and united church. Such engagement with diverse prayer communities is more than just an exercise in spiritual growth; it's a step towards actualizing the unity for which Jesus prayed – a unity that reflects His love and draws others to Him. Let our participation in these groups be a journey of discovery, fellowship, and transformation, as we grow in our understanding of God and of each other, weaving together our prayers in a harmonious chorus that ascends to the throne of grace.

Fellowship with Different Cultures

In the unfolding story of our faith journey, actively seeking fellowship with people from different cultures stands as a vital chapter, rich in learning and growth. It's a chapter where the palette of our experiences broadens, colored by the diverse hues of cultures different from our own. This endeavor is more than an exploration; it's a conscious effort to weave the unique experiences of various cultures into our understanding of humanity, strengthening our appreciation for the beauty of God's creation and revealing the universal values and aspirations that bind us together as His children.

Imagine embarking on a global expedition without leaving your city – a journey that takes you through the heart of different cultures. This journey involves participating in cultural events, trying new foods, learning about different customs and traditions, and spending time in conversation with people from various backgrounds. It's an adventure that not only enriches your understanding of the world but also deepens your appreciation for the diversity within God's Kingdom.

The Bible often speaks about the beauty and strength found in diversity. In Revelation 7:9, John describes a vision of heaven: "After this I looked, and there before me was a great multitude that no one could count, from every nation, tribe, people and language, standing before the throne and before the Lamb." This scripture paints a picture of a heavenly gathering enriched by cultural diversity, united in worship and praise. It reminds us that our endeavor to connect with different cultures mirrors the diversity that exists within God's Kingdom.

Participating in cultural events and festivals is a wonderful way to immerse oneself in different traditions. It's an opportunity to celebrate the uniqueness of each culture while recognizing the shared sense of joy, community, and belonging that such events evoke. Trying new foods from various cultures is not just a culinary adventure but a foray into the history, geography, and soul of a people. Food often tells a story, and sharing a meal is a universal expression of hospitality and friendship.

Conversations with people from diverse backgrounds can be incredibly enlightening. These dialogues open windows into different worldviews, offering insights into how others perceive life, faith, and community. They challenge our preconceptions and broaden our understanding of what it means to walk in faith. As we listen to the stories of others, we are reminded of the Apostle Paul's words in Romans 12:15-16, "Rejoice with those who rejoice; mourn with those who mourn. Live in harmony with one another."

In our interactions with different cultures, we often find that despite the diversity in practices and beliefs, there are universal themes that resonate with all – themes of love, family, faith, hope, and the pursuit of happiness. These common threads underscore our shared humanity, reminding us that we are more alike than we are different.

Moreover, fellowship with different cultures is an exercise in empathy and understanding. It's about seeing the world through the eyes of others, appreciating their struggles, celebrating their achievements, and learning from their wisdom. In doing so, we reflect the character of Christ, who showed love and compassion to all, regardless of their cultural background.

This engagement with diverse cultures also helps to dispel stereotypes and break down barriers of misunderstanding. It fosters an environment of mutual respect and unity, qualities that are essential in building a strong and vibrant church community.

As Kingdom Citizens, we are called to be ambassadors of Christ's love and grace to all people. This means stepping out of our cultural comfort zones and reaching out to others with genuine interest and humility. It's about building bridges of understanding and friendship, transcending cultural divides.

In conclusion, as we pursue fellowship with different cultures, let's do so with open hearts and minds. Let us seize every opportunity to learn, share, and grow through our interactions with others. Let's celebrate the diversity that God has woven into the fabric of humanity, recognizing that in each culture lies a unique reflection of His creativity and love. Through these engagements, we not only enrich our own lives but also contribute to the building of a church and a world that truly reflects the unity and diversity of God's Kingdom. Let our fellowship with different cultures be a journey of discovery and transformation, as we seek to understand and appreciate the myriad ways in which God reveals Himself to His people across the globe.

Travel and Visit Other Countries

Traveling to and visiting other countries is akin to opening a book full of vibrant stories, each page rich with the possibility of new insights, challenges, and learnings. This form of engagement with diversity is not merely a journey across physical distances; it is a transformative experience that exposes us to new ways of living, thinking, and believing. It's an expedition that can profoundly shift our preconceptions, broaden our worldview, and foster within us a deeper empathy and understanding as global citizens. This chapter of our journey in embracing diversity is a vivid exploration of the vast and wonderful canvas of God's creation, showcasing the incredible variety and beauty inherent within it.

Imagine stepping off a plane and being immediately enveloped by the sights, sounds, and smells of a new country. Here, the rhythm of life is different, the language unfamiliar, the customs intriguing. Each moment is an opportunity to learn and grow. Whether wandering through bustling markets, observing local rituals, or engaging in conversations with the locals, each experience is a doorway to deeper understanding and appreciation of a culture distinct from our own.

In the heart of these travels, we find ourselves continually confronted with our own preconceptions and biases. Like the disciples, who were challenged to embrace different cultures and people in their missionary journeys, we too are called to step out of our comfort zones and engage with the world around us. Acts 1:8 says, "You will receive power when the Holy Spirit comes on you; and you will be my witnesses in Jerusalem, and in all Judea and Samaria, and to the ends of the earth." Traveling to other countries is a way of living out this call, witnessing the breadth and depth of God's work in diverse settings.

As we journey through different lands, we not only encounter new cultural landscapes but also discover the universal human experiences that connect us all. We find common ground in shared joys, struggles, and aspirations, even as we navigate the uniqueness of each place and people. This commonality in the human experience is a powerful reminder of God's love for all His creation, transcending geographical, cultural, and linguistic barriers.

Moreover, travel often leads to moments of profound spiritual reflection and growth. In experiencing the majesty of God's creation – from towering mountains and expansive oceans to the intricate details of art and architecture – we gain a renewed sense of awe and wonder at His creativity and power. Psalms 24:1 reminds us, "The earth is the Lord's, and everything in it, the world, and all who live in it." In traveling, we see the truth of this verse unfold before our eyes, as we witness the diversity and beauty of the world He has made.

Traveling also fosters empathy and understanding. As we step into the lives of others, even for a brief moment, we begin to understand their perspectives and experiences. This empathy is vital in a world that is often divided by misunderstandings and lack of knowledge about 'the other.' It's a step towards fulfilling the call to love our neighbors as ourselves, a principle that lies at the heart of Jesus' teachings.

Traveling and visiting other countries is an invaluable experience in the quest to embrace diversity. It's an adventure that challenges and changes us, expanding our understanding of the world and its people. As we immerse ourselves in new cultures and experiences, let us do so with open hearts and minds, ready to learn, grow, and be transformed. Let our travels not just be about seeing new places, but about gaining new perspectives – perspectives that enrich our understanding of God's creation and deepen our compassion for our fellow humans. In this journey across borders, let us embrace the diversity and richness of the world, becoming more empathetic, informed, and connected citizens of this global community.

United We Stand, Divided We Fall

In the grand narrative of God's Kingdom, the principle of unity holds a place of profound significance. "United We Stand, Divided

We Fall," a phrase echoed throughout history, resonates with even greater depth in the context of our faith. This final section of Chapter 4: "Embracing Diversity," is a powerful reminder that our commitment to diversity is not merely a noble ideal, but a practical imperative for forging a strong, united, and effective community under God's sovereignty. The richness of diversity within the Body of Christ is a treasure to be celebrated and leveraged – a source of strength, resilience, and dynamic effectiveness in fulfilling our collective purpose in God's grand design.

Picture a vibrant garden where every plant, flower, and tree thrives in its unique way, contributing to the garden's overall health and beauty. Each species brings something special – be it shade, fragrance, or color – that enriches the garden's ecosystem. This garden is a living metaphor for a diverse yet united community, where our differences in background, culture, and perspective not only coexist but synergistically contribute to the flourishing of the whole.

The Apostle Paul speaks to this in 1 Corinthians 12:12-27, using the human body as an analogy for the church. He illustrates how each part, though different, is essential to the body's functionality and unity. In a similar way, each member of the Kingdom community, with their unique gifts and backgrounds, is vital to the health and effectiveness of the whole. In our diversity, we find a broader range of skills, experiences, and perspectives that, when united, create a formidable force in the advancement of God's Kingdom.

Embracing diversity and fostering unity is not just about coexisting peacefully; it's about actively working together, valuing each other's contributions, and supporting one another. It's about recognizing that in our differences lie our strengths. When we come together – combining our various gifts, insights, and passions – we create a mosaic that is far more capable and resilient than any of us could be alone.

Moreover, our unity amidst diversity serves as a powerful testament to the world of the reconciling and inclusive nature of God's Kingdom. Jesus prayed for this unity in John 17:21-23, expressing His desire that all believers be one, just as He and the Father are one. This unity was not for unity's sake alone, but so that the world might believe in the truth of the Gospel. Our united stance, therefore, is a compelling witness to the power and love of God, demonstrating the reality of the Gospel in a tangible and impactful way.

The journey towards embracing diversity and fostering unity may have its challenges. It requires humility, patience, and a willingness to listen and learn from one another. But the rewards are immense. United in our diversity, we become more resilient in the face of trials, more creative in our problem-solving, and more effective in our mission.

In conclusion, as we close this chapter, let us be inspired to seek and celebrate diversity within our communities. Let us strive for unity, not uniformity, understanding that our collective strength lies in our ability to harness the rich variety of gifts God has bestowed upon us. Let us embrace our differences, recognizing them as opportunities for growth, enrichment, and more profound connection. In doing so, we not only build a stronger, more vibrant community but also exemplify the heart of the Gospel – a message of reconciliation, unity, and love that transcends all barriers. United in our diversity, we stand as a living testimony to the power and grace of God, showcasing to the world the beauty and strength that is found when we come together as one body in Christ.

As we draw the curtains on Chapter 4, we do so with a renewed sense of purpose and a profound realization. This journey through the theme of embracing diversity has not just broadened our perspectives; it has deeply enriched our understanding of God's character and His Kingdom. Embracing diversity goes beyond appreciating it as a mere concept; it's about living it out as a powerful testament to God's inclusive and reconciling nature, a testament that richly enhances our collective experience within His Kingdom.

Throughout this chapter, we have traversed various landscapes of human interaction, from the intimacy of local community groups to the expansive experiences of international travel. In each setting, we've discovered the inherent beauty and strength that diversity brings to our shared journey in faith. We've seen how our differences – in culture, background, and perspective – rather than being divisions, are unique threads in the rich fabric of our communal life in Christ.

In engaging with and learning from each other's diverse experiences, we reflect the manifold wisdom and creativity of God. Each interaction, each shared story, each cultural exchange has revealed a facet of His divine tapestry. These encounters have not only expanded our view of the world but also deepened our appreciation for the myriad ways in which God works in and through His people.

This chapter has also called us to practical action in embracing diversity. It has urged us to step out of our comfort zones and engage meaningfully with the diversity that surrounds us. This involves listening, learning, and growing in our understanding of each other, recognizing that every individual is a bearer of God's image and a reflection of His diversity.

As we conclude this chapter, we carry with us the inspiration to see diversity not merely as a concept but as a lived experience, one that enriches our collective journey in God's Kingdom. Our daily interactions become opportunities to practice this understanding, to embrace the richness that each unique individual brings to our community.

Embracing diversity is an ongoing journey of discovery, insight, and connection. It requires an openness to new experiences, a willingness to be transformed, and a heart that seeks to understand and celebrate the diversity that God has woven into the very fabric of creation.

Therefore, as we move forward from Chapter 4, let us do so with a commitment to embody the inclusive and reconciling nature of God's Kingdom. Let us strive to build communities that reflect the beauty and variety of His universal church – diverse in composition, united in purpose, and abundant in love.

In this light, we end Chapter 4 with a heart full of gratitude for the diversity that enriches our lives, ready to embrace and celebrate the vast, beautiful landscape of humanity that is an integral part of our life in God's Kingdom.

Chapter 5

The Role of Empathy

In this pivotal chapter, "The Role of Empathy," we delve into the profound significance of empathy in cultivating relationships that not only thrive on a human level but are also rooted in the divine vision of the Kingdom. Empathy, as we will explore, is more than a mere emotional response; it is a fundamental component in the architecture of meaningful Kingdom relationships. By seeing others through God's lens, we can deepen our understanding and connections, thereby paving the way for genuine unity and a stronger communal fabric.

The concept of empathy in the context of Kingdom relationships involves a heartfelt and sincere effort to understand and share the feelings of others. It requires us to step outside our own experiences and perspectives, to inhabit, as much as we can, the lives of those around us. This chapter will explore how this kind of empathetic engagement is not just beneficial but essential for building strong, lasting relationships. Empathy allows us to connect with others on a deeper level, fostering an environment where love, understanding, and mutual respect flourish.

Empathy in Kingdom relationships is not merely about emotional resonance; it's about active listening, understanding, and responding in a manner that reflects God's love and compassion. We will explore biblical examples and teachings that emphasize the importance of empathy in our interactions. Jesus Christ himself exemplified this profound empathy in his ministry, where he consistently showed deep understanding and compassion for the plight, struggles, and joys of those he encountered.

However, cultivating empathy is not without its challenges. In a world where differences often lead to division, empathy can be the bridge that connects diverse experiences and viewpoints. This chapter will address the barriers to empathy, such as preconceived notions, biases, and the distractions of our fast-paced, often superficial modern life. We will discuss practical strategies for overcoming these obstacles, emphasizing the importance of mindfulness, active listening, and the intentional practice of placing oneself in another's shoes.

Moreover, this chapter will highlight the transformative power of empathy in conflict resolution within the Kingdom community. Empathy does not mean always agreeing with others but rather understanding where they are coming from. This understanding can lead to more compassionate, effective ways of resolving disagreements, thereby strengthening the bonds within the community.

Empathy extends beyond individual relationships; it has a collective dimension. When practiced widely, empathy can lead to a more compassionate society, reflecting the Kingdom's values of love, peace, and unity. By fostering empathy, we contribute to a world where everyone feels understood, valued, and connected.

"The Role of Empathy" aims to inspire and guide readers towards cultivating deeper, more empathetic relationships. Through scriptural insights, practical advice, and reflective exercises, this chapter serves as a roadmap for anyone seeking to build stronger, more meaningful connections in their personal lives and within their communities. As we journey through this chapter, let us embrace the power of empathy in forging relationships that embody the love, unity, and purpose God has destined for us.

We Must See Others Through God's Perspective

In the heart of Kingdom Building lies a profound and transformative principle: to see others through God's perspective. This vision extends beyond mere observation; it's an invitation to understand and connect with people from all walks of life, embodying the core value of empathy. To empathize is to share in the feelings and experiences of others, and this chapter delves into how this vital attribute enriches our relationships, nurtures our communities, and aligns us with God's purpose.

Imagine walking through a bustling market in a distant land, surrounded by the vibrancy of cultures vastly different from your own. In this setting, empathy becomes the bridge that connects your heart to the hearts of those around you. Each interaction, each smile exchanged, and each story shared is an opportunity to see the world through another's eyes, to understand their joys, their struggles, and their dreams. It's a moment to reflect upon the Apostle Paul's words in Romans 12:15, "Rejoice with those who rejoice; mourn with those who mourn." This scripture vividly illustrates the essence of empathy — participating wholeheartedly in the emotional journeys of others.

Empathy in Kingdom Building, therefore, is not a passive experience; it's an active, deliberate pursuit of heartfelt understanding and connection. It's about celebrating the diversity God has created and recognizing the unique contributions each individual brings to the tapestry of life. As we encounter different cultures, traditions, and perspectives, we are presented with a rich palette of experiences that can deepen our understanding of humanity and, more importantly, of God's infinite creativity and love.

Consider the story of the Good Samaritan, a powerful parable told by Jesus in Luke 10:25-37. Here, Jesus challenges societal norms and prejudices by highlighting a Samaritan's act of kindness towards a Jew, someone considered an enemy. This story transcends cultural barriers, teaching us that true empathy does not discriminate; it sees beyond ethnicity, social status, and historical conflicts. It speaks directly to our calling to love our neighbors as ourselves, as emphasized in Mark 12:31.

To cultivate such empathy requires us to step out of our comfort zones and immerse ourselves in the lives and cultures of others. It means sitting down with people from different backgrounds, listening to their stories, understanding their viewpoints, and finding common ground. Through this process, we not only grow in our appreciation of diversity but also in our capacity to love as Christ loves us — unconditionally and without prejudice.

In Kingdom Building, empathy also plays a critical role in mission and evangelism. By empathizing with those we seek to reach, we can better understand their needs, fears, and hopes. This understanding enables us to share the Gospel in a way that resonates deeply with their individual experiences. In 1 Corinthians 9:22, Paul speaks to this adaptive approach in ministry, "I have become all things to all people so that by all possible means I might save some." This verse encapsulates the essence of empathetic outreach — adapting to and respecting the cultures and contexts of those we serve.

But empathy in Kingdom Building is not without its challenges. We live in a world where differences are often amplified and used to divide. Empathy calls us to bridge these divides, to find unity in diversity, and to see each person as a cherished creation of God, imbued with dignity and worth. It invites us to journey alongside others, sharing in their triumphs and their trials, and in doing so, reflect the inclusive and encompassing love of Christ.

Embracing empathy in Kingdom Building is a journey of the heart. It's about seeing others through God's perspective, recognizing the image of God in everyone we meet. As we embark on this journey, let us be guided by the words of Philippians 2:4, "Let each of you look not only to his own interests, but also to the interests of others." This is the heart of empathy — a heart that sees, understands, and loves as God does. Through empathy, we can forge connections that transcend cultural boundaries, enrich our spiritual lives, and fulfill our calling to build God's Kingdom on Earth.

Get to Know and Understand the Strengths and Weaknesses of Those You Partner With

Building meaningful relationships within the Kingdom requires us to delve deeply into the lives of those we partner with. This exploration is akin to treading a path filled with diverse landscapes, each revealing the distinct contours of an individual's strengths and weaknesses. It's a journey that calls for patience, insight, and an open heart, aiming to build a community where everyone's unique contributions are valued, and their challenges met with understanding and support.

Imagine a mosaic of lives, each tile representing a person with whom we share our journey of faith and life. One might be the bright, vibrant piece, full of energy and charisma, naturally gifted in leadership and inspiring those around them. Yet, this same individual might struggle with the quieter moments, finding it challenging to listen and reflect. Another tile might be softer, more subtle in color, depicting someone with a deep capacity for listening and empathy, but who may grapple with self-doubt or fear of speaking out.

The biblical story of Paul and Timothy serves as a poignant illustration of this understanding. Paul, a seasoned apostle, recognized the potential in young Timothy, his strengths in faith and dedication. However, Paul also acknowledged Timothy's youth and the apprehensions that accompanied it, as reflected in his letters encouraging Timothy to not let anyone look down on him because of his youth (1 Timothy 4:12). This mentorship exemplifies how recognizing and supporting each other's strengths and weaknesses can lead to growth and empowerment within the Kingdom.

In getting to know those we partner with, it's essential to spend time in their presence, to share in their experiences and listen to their stories. It's about creating spaces where individuals feel comfortable unveiling the layers of their lives - the bright and the dim, the strong and the vulnerable. Such spaces are reminiscent of the early Christian communities, where believers met regularly, breaking bread in their homes, and sharing their lives with glad and sincere hearts (Acts 2:46).

Understanding someone's strengths allows us to lean on them, to be inspired and guided by their gifts. It's an opportunity to celebrate their capabilities and encourage them to shine in their areas of expertise. Just as the body has many parts, each with its unique function (1 Corinthians 12:12-27), so too in the community of faith, each member brings distinct talents that contribute to the common good.

Conversely, recognizing someone's weaknesses is not about highlighting their flaws but about understanding their human nature and extending grace. It's an invitation to walk alongside them, offering support, encouragement, and sometimes gentle correction. This approach reflects the heart of Jesus' teachings – to bear one another's burdens, fulfilling the law of Christ (Galatians 6:2). It's about building a community where everyone feels seen, heard, and valued, irrespective of their limitations.

This journey of understanding is not without its challenges. It requires patience, humility, and a willingness to sometimes put our own perspectives aside. However, the rewards are immeasurable.

By truly knowing those we partner with, by understanding their strengths and weaknesses, we build a stronger, more cohesive community. We create an environment where each member can thrive, contribute their best, and, in turn, help others to do the same.

The first step in cultivating empathy within the Kingdom is a commitment to genuinely knowing those we share our journey with. It's about recognizing and valuing the unique tapestry of talents and challenges each person brings. This understanding fosters a nurturing and supportive environment, essential for the growth and flourishing of individual members and the community as a whole. As we journey together, let us remember that in Christ, we are many parts of one body, each indispensable and deeply valued.

Share Your Strengths and Weaknesses

In the dynamic interplay of relationships within the Kingdom, empathy emerges not just as an act of understanding others, but also as a practice of openness about ourselves. To share our strengths and weaknesses is to invite others into our own journey, painting a picture of who we truly are - a canvas marked by both bright strokes of talent and shadowed areas of vulnerability. This section of Chapter 5 is a call to embrace this vulnerability, to create a culture where transparency and trust flourish, leading to a community that is not only authentic but deeply supportive.

Imagine a circle of friends, gathered around a warm fire, each taking turns to share stories from their lives. One speaks of a recent success, a moment where their strength shone brightly, igniting inspiration in the others. Another shares a story of struggle, a time when their weakness was evident, and their need for support was great. This circle represents the essence of a community where empathy is a two-way street, a place where the sharing of both triumphs and trials is not just accepted but encouraged.

The biblical narrative offers us a compelling example in the relationship between David and Jonathan. Jonathan, recognizing David's strengths, supported and protected him, even though it meant challenging his own father, King Saul (1 Samuel 18:1-4). Yet, there were moments when David, despite his many strengths, revealed his vulnerabilities, such as in his psalms where he poured out his fears and doubts before God. Their relationship exemplifies a mutual sharing of strengths and weaknesses, forming a bond of deep trust and respect.

Sharing our strengths is a way of offering our gifts for the benefit of others, just as the parable of the talents teaches us to utilize our God-given abilities for the growth of the Kingdom (Matthew 25:14-30). It's about stepping forward, bringing our best to the table, and uplifting the community. Our strengths, when shared, become a source of inspiration and guidance for others, a beacon that illuminates the path for those walking alongside us.

Conversely, sharing our weaknesses is equally important. It requires humility and courage, for it involves exposing the parts of ourselves that are often hidden. Yet, in doing so, we create a space for genuine connection and understanding. We remind others that it's okay to be imperfect, to have areas that need growth. This act of vulnerability is beautifully reflected in Paul's words, "My grace is sufficient for you, for my power is made perfect in weakness" (2 Corinthians 12:9). Paul's admission of his struggles and his reliance on God's strength is a powerful testament to the value of embracing our vulnerabilities.

By sharing our weaknesses, we also invite others to walk with us, to offer their strengths in areas where we may falter. This creates a culture of mutual support and interdependence, mirroring the early Christian community where believers cared for one another, sharing their possessions and burdens (Acts 2:44-45).

The sharing of our strengths and weaknesses is not just about individual expression; it's about building a community where every member feels valued and understood. It's about creating an environment where each person can be authentic, without fear of judgment, and where the collective strength of the community is fortified by the unique contributions of each individual.

In conclusion, the practice of sharing our strengths and weaknesses is a vital step in cultivating empathy and building a supportive, authentic community. It's a journey that calls for bravery, honesty, and a willingness to be seen in our entirety. As we embrace this practice, we not only strengthen our bonds with one another but also enrich the fabric of the community we are part of. In doing so, we reflect the heart of the Gospel - a message of love, acceptance, and mutual edification - and move closer to realizing the vision of the Kingdom here on Earth.

Commit to Uplifting Others

In the heart of empathy lies a luminous commitment - a dedication to uplift others. This commitment, an essential facet of Kingdom building, is akin to nurturing a garden where each plant is tended to with care, ensuring it receives enough sunlight, water, and nutrients to flourish. In our relationships, this means actively seeking ways to encourage, support, and edify those around us, creating an environment where every individual can grow and thrive.

Envision a scene where a seasoned gardener walks through their garden. They pause by each plant, assessing its needs, offering water to those that are thirsty, support to the ones that are drooping, and pruning the ones that need it. This is the essence of uplifting others - understanding and responding to their needs in a way that encourages growth and resilience.

The story of Barnabas in the Acts of the Apostles serves as a splendid illustration of this commitment. Known as the 'Son of Encouragement', Barnabas stood by Paul when he was a new convert, despite the skepticism and fear of other believers (Acts 9:27). He saw the potential in Paul and advocated for him, helping him become one of the most influential figures in Christian history. Barnabas also supported John Mark, despite his initial shortcomings (Acts 15:37-39). His actions epitomize the power of encouragement and the significant impact it can have on an individual's life and the broader community.

Uplifting others can take many forms, from words of affirmation that instill confidence and hope to acts of service that ease burdens. It can be as simple as a listening ear, offering our presence and attention in a world where both are increasingly scarce. Every act of encouragement is a ripple in the pond, capable of spreading far beyond its initial impact.

Consider the power of positive words, as mentioned in Proverbs 16:24, "Gracious words are a honeycomb, sweet to the soul and healing to the bones." Encouraging words can be a source of strength and comfort, lifting spirits and nurturing hope. They remind us of the affirmations Jesus himself gave to those he encountered, acknowledging their faith, their struggles, and their worth.

Similarly, acts of service, whether grand or modest, are expressions of Christ's love and compassion. In Matthew 25:40, Jesus said, "Truly I tell you, whatever you did for one of the least of these brothers and sisters of mine, you did for me." Through our actions, we can manifest the tangible love of Christ, supporting and uplifting those in need.

Committing to uplift others also means being a listening ear. In the story of Job, after his friends' initial attempt to explain his suffering, they simply sat with him in silence, sharing in his pain (Job 2:13). Sometimes, the best way to uplift someone is just by being there, offering our presence as a comfort and a support.

This commitment to uplifting others is not only a blessing to those we support but also enriches our own lives. It strengthens the bonds within our community, creating a network of support and encouragement. As we each contribute to uplifting one another, we build a stronger, more resilient community, reflective of the love and compassion of Christ.

The commitment to uplift others is a vital expression of empathy in our relationships. It calls for us to be attentive, caring, and proactive in our support of one another. Through words of affirmation, acts of service, and being a listening ear, we reflect the love of Christ and strengthen our community. Let us embrace this commitment, nurturing a culture where everyone is encouraged to grow, supported in their struggles, and celebrated in their achievements. In doing so, we honor the essence of the Kingdom and manifest the transformative power of Christ's love.

Allow Others to Uplift You

In the symphony of relationships that orchestrate the Kingdom, there's a melody that often goes unheard - the gentle hum of allowing others to uplift us. This melody sings of humility, openness, and the recognition of our interconnectedness in Christ. It's a vital counterpoint to our commitment to uplift others, for in the ebb and flow of giving and receiving support, we find a harmony that strengthens not only our individual spirits but the collective soul of our community.

Picture a skilled climber, always ready to offer a hand to help others ascend the mountain's challenging face. Yet, when they find themselves on a precarious ledge, unsure of the next step, the true test comes in accepting a guiding hand from their fellow climbers. This is the essence of allowing others to uplift us - acknowledging that despite our strengths, there are moments when we too need assistance to climb higher.

The biblical narrative is rich with examples of this mutual support. Moses, a leader par excellence, found his arms growing weary during a crucial battle. It was Aaron and Hur who held up his arms, providing the support he needed to ensure victory for the Israelites (Exodus 17:12). In this moment, Moses' openness to receiving help was as crucial as his leadership. It showed that even the mightiest among us have moments of need.

Allowing others to uplift us requires humility, an acknowledgment that we are not islands unto ourselves, but part of a larger body. It's about shedding the illusion of self-sufficiency and embracing the strength that comes from being interconnected in the Body of Christ. Paul's words in 2 Corinthians 12:9 resonate deeply here, "My grace is sufficient for you, for my power is made perfect in weakness." Admitting our need for support is not a sign of weakness, but a testament to our reliance on God's grace, working through the hands and hearts of our brothers and sisters.

Embracing the support of others can manifest in various ways. It might be through the encouraging words of a friend that lift us during times of doubt, or the wise counsel of a mentor that guides us when we face crossroads. It could be the simple act of someone being present, sharing our burdens, as seen in the support Job received from his friends who sat with him in his time of suffering (Job 2:13).

The act of allowing others to uplift us also nurtures a culture of vulnerability and trust within our communities. When we openly accept support, we signal to others that it's okay to be in need, to rely on each other. This creates a ripple effect, encouraging a community where members feel safe to expose their struggles, knowing they will be met with compassion and aid.

Moreover, allowing ourselves to be uplifted is an act of faith, a trust in God's provision through the community. It's a recognition that the Lord often works through His people, providing us with the strength, wisdom, and comfort we need through the hands and hearts of those around us.

Allowing others to uplift us is a crucial aspect of our journey in the Kingdom. It's a dance of give-and-take, a balance of offering support and accepting it. This reciprocal uplifting fosters a community where every member is both a pillar of strength and a recipient of grace. As we learn to open our hearts and let others in, we not only strengthen our bonds but also embody the essence of Christ's teachings - to bear one another's burdens and so fulfill the law of love. In this shared strength and vulnerability, we find the true power of our community in Christ, a place where every member is valued, supported, and uplifted.

Embrace Other People's Perspectives

Each individual's perspective is like a unique vantage point on a vast mountain range. From each spot, the view is different, shaped by the contours of personal experiences, beliefs, and emotions. Embracing other people's perspectives is like journeying to these various outlooks, not to change our position but to broaden our horizon. This chapter leads us through the paths of empathy, where understanding divergent viewpoints isn't about compromising our beliefs but about enriching our comprehension of the human condition.

Picture a group of pilgrims, each coming from different directions, gathering around a sacred site. They share stories of their journeys - the paths they've taken, the landscapes they've crossed, and the challenges they've faced. Each story is different, yet each is true and valid in its own right. This gathering represents the beauty of embracing diverse perspectives. It's not about whose path is correct, but about understanding that each path has its own trials and triumphs, and each leads to the same destination.

The story of Jesus and the Samaritan woman at the well (John 4:1-26) is a profound example of embracing perspectives. Jesus, a Jew, engages in conversation with a Samaritan woman, an act that transcends deep-rooted cultural and gender prejudices of that time. He listens to her, acknowledges her life experiences, and speaks into her situation, leading to a transformation not just in her but in her entire community. This interaction underscores the power of understanding and valuing the perspectives of others, even when they vastly differ from our own.

Listening with an open heart and mind is fundamental in embracing other perspectives. It's about quieting our inner voices and preconceptions to truly hear what others are saying. This kind of listening is exemplified in the biblical practice of "Shema," a Hebrew word meaning to hear or listen deeply (Deuteronomy 6:4-5). It's a listening that goes beyond the surface, seeking to understand the heart of what is being communicated.

Acknowledging the validity of others' feelings and experiences is equally crucial. It requires a certain humility, a willingness to accept that our view of the world is not the only one. Proverbs 18:2 reminds us, "Fools find no pleasure in understanding but delight in airing their own opinions." True wisdom lies in seeking understanding, in valuing the insights that come from diverse experiences.

Learning from different perspectives enriches us. It allows us to see the world through the eyes of others, to empathize with their joys and sorrows, and to gain insights that we might have missed from our viewpoint. This learning is not about diluting our beliefs, but about deepening our understanding of life and faith.

The act of embracing diverse perspectives fosters deeper connections within our communities. It creates a space where everyone feels heard and valued, a community that reflects the inclusivity and empathy of Christ. As we walk in the footsteps of Jesus, let us strive to listen, acknowledge, and learn from the myriad of perspectives around us.

Embracing other people's perspectives is a journey of the heart, a path towards a more inclusive and empathetic community. It's a commitment to understanding and valuing the diverse experiences and views of those around us. This journey not only brings us closer to others but also closer to the heart of the Kingdom, where every voice is heard, every story is valued, and every perspective is cherished. As we continue to walk this path, let us do so with open hearts and minds, ready to embrace the rich tapestry of human experience that God has woven in His creation.

In a Healthy Relationship, There Should Never Be Any Partiality

In the expanse of human interactions, healthy, God-centered relationships stand as beacons of hope and harmony, illuminating the path to a world where love and empathy reign supreme. In these relationships, partiality has no place; instead, the lens of God's love and grace brings every individual into sharp, equal focus. Through the lens of empathy, we see not just with our eyes, but with our hearts, breaking down the walls of misunderstanding and judgment and building bridges of genuine connection.

Picture a garden where a variety of flowers bloom in harmony, each unique in its beauty yet equally cherished by the gardener. This garden is a metaphor for healthy relationships in the Kingdom of God, where every person is valued, and no one is favored or marginalized. In this garden, the sun shines equally on all, representing the love and grace of God that encompasses every individual without partiality.

The scriptural parable of the Good Samaritan (Luke 10:25-37) provides a compelling illustration of this principle. In this story, a man is left wounded on the roadside, and while others pass him by, a Samaritan, considered an outsider and enemy by many, stops to help. This Samaritan's actions were not influenced by societal biases or prejudices. He saw the wounded man not through the lens of race or status but through the lens of common humanity and compassion. His actions epitomize the essence of empathy and the call to love our neighbors as ourselves, transcending the boundaries of partiality.

Empathy in healthy relationships means actively striving to understand and appreciate the experiences and perspectives of others, regardless of their background, status, or beliefs. It's about listening deeply, speaking kindly, and acting justly. James 2:1 warns against showing favoritism, reminding us that God's love is impartial and that we are called to reflect this divine attribute in our relationships.

In a world rife with divisions and biases, the Church is tasked with setting a higher standard – one of unconditional love, understanding, and empathy. This is not always an easy path, as it requires confronting and challenging our preconceptions and biases. Yet, it is a journey worth taking, for it leads to the creation of a community where every member feels valued and respected.

The early Christian community exemplified this principle. In Acts 10, Peter, a Jew, had a vision that led him to Cornelius, a Gentile, breaking the traditional barriers of religious and cultural partiality. This encounter was a significant step in the early church, demonstrating that the message of Jesus was for all humanity, not confined by the boundaries of race or culture.

Embracing empathy and eschewing partiality in our relationships fosters a sense of belonging and unity. It creates a space where individuals can share their stories, their struggles, and their triumphs, knowing they will be met with open hearts and minds. In this environment, the unique experiences and perspectives of each person contribute to the collective wisdom and strength of the community.

In conclusion, empathy is the cornerstone of healthy, God-centered relationships. It requires us to see each person through God's lens of love and grace, recognizing the intrinsic value and worth of every individual. By breaking down barriers of misunderstanding and judgment, empathy paves the way for genuine connections and a community where everyone is equally valued and cherished. As we strive to live out this principle, let us remember that in the Kingdom of God, there is no room for partiality – only a profound and all-encompassing love that binds us together in unity and understanding.

Now, we are reminded of the transformative power of empathy. It stands as a pivotal force, not just in sculpting healthy, God-centered relationships but in fostering an environment where spiritual unity flourishes. Empathy, in its purest form, is an embodiment of Christ's love — a love that sees beyond the surface, reaches into the depths of human experience, and connects soul to soul.

Throughout this chapter, we have journeyed through various landscapes of empathy. We began by understanding the importance of seeing others through God's perspective, recognizing that every individual is a unique creation, worthy of love and understanding. We then explored the necessity of embracing each person's strengths and weaknesses, realizing that in the interplay of these traits lies the beauty of our shared humanity. By sharing our own vulnerabilities and strengths, we contribute to a culture of transparency and trust, which is essential for any thriving community.

We delved into the commitment to uplifting others and the humility in allowing others to uplift us, finding that in these acts of giving and receiving, the bonds of fellowship are strengthened. In embracing diverse perspectives, we widen our horizons, enriching our understanding and compassion. Finally, we addressed the importance of eschewing partiality, emphasizing that in a world often divided by differences, our call to empathy is a call to unite in the love and grace of God.

In conclusion, empathy is not merely an emotional response; it is a deliberate choice and a spiritual discipline that aligns our hearts with the heart of God. It challenges us to look beyond ourselves, to see the world through a lens of grace and compassion. As we close this chapter, let us carry forward the lessons learned, making empathy a cornerstone in our daily interactions and relationships. By doing so, we not only build stronger, more genuine connections but also inch closer to the spiritual unity that is so profoundly desired in the Kingdom of God.

Chapter 6

Financial Unity

As we embark on Chapter 6, "Financial Unity," we delve into a critical yet often overlooked aspect of Kingdom Building: the powerful role of financial collaboration. This chapter opens a discourse on the synergy that financial unity can bring, not just in terms of resource pooling, but as a fundamental pillar in strengthening the bonds of our community and propelling our shared mission forward. In a world where financial matters often lead to division and discord, the principle of financial unity stands as a beacon of hope and cooperation.

Financial unity in the context of Kingdom Building is more than a mere congregation of resources; it's a reflection of our shared values, goals, and visions. It involves a collective mindset where members view their financial contributions not as mere transactions, but as investments into a common vision. This concept is rooted deeply in the New Testament, where the early Christians practiced communal living, sharing everything they had for the benefit of all (Acts 2:44-45). It was an extraordinary display of unity and generosity, where financial resources were pooled to meet the needs of every member, ensuring that no one among them was in lack.

However, achieving financial unity is not without its challenges. It requires transparency, trust, and a commitment to mutual support and accountability. It calls for a shift from a perspective of individual ownership to a recognition that all we have is a stewardship from God, to be used wisely for the advancement of His Kingdom. As we navigate through this chapter, we explore practical ways in which communities can cultivate a culture of financial unity, guided by biblical principles and real-world examples.

The practice of tithing, for instance, is not merely a religious obligation, but a testament to our trust in God's provision and our commitment to support the collective mission of the church. The act of giving, as encouraged in 2 Corinthians 9:7 – "Each of you should give what you have decided in your heart to give, not reluctantly or under compulsion, for God loves a cheerful giver," – is a vital part of our worship and a reflection of our heart's posture towards God and our community.

This chapter also addresses the impact of financial unity on community outreach and mission work. Financial collaboration enables the church to extend its reach beyond its walls, impacting communities, supporting missions, and aiding those in need. It is an embodiment of the biblical call to be the hands and feet of Jesus in a world in need of His love and grace.

Furthermore, we discuss the importance of financial education within the community. A common understanding of financial management, generosity, and stewardship can lead to more effective use of resources, reducing the likelihood of conflicts and fostering a spirit of unity and cooperation.

In conclusion, financial unity is a key component in the fabric of Kingdom Building. It's a manifestation of our faith in action, where each contribution, big or small, weaves together to form a strong, supportive network that uplifts the entire community. As we journey through this chapter, let us be inspired to view our financial resources not just as personal assets, but as tools for building a stronger, more unified community, advancing the Kingdom of God on Earth.

Be Willing to Sow and Invest into The Kingdom Financially

At the heart of financial unity lies a powerful and transformative concept: the willingness to sow and invest into the Kingdom of God. This notion extends far beyond mere monetary transactions; it's an act of faith, a declaration of our commitment to the collective vision and mission of the Kingdom. Throughout this chapter, we explore this dynamic aspect of Kingdom Building, where each financial contribution becomes a seed sown into fertile ground, promising a harvest of collective prosperity and strengthened community bonds.

Envision a farmer tending to his fields, meticulously sowing seeds with the hope and expectation of a bountiful harvest. This image mirrors our financial contributions to the Kingdom of God. Each dollar given is like a seed planted in the soil of God's work — it holds the potential for growth, multiplication, and a profound impact beyond its initial size. The act of giving financially is thus an exercise in faith and hope, rooted in the promises of God.

The biblical principle of sowing and reaping, as outlined in 2 Corinthians 9:6-7, powerfully encapsulates this concept: "Whoever sows sparingly will also reap sparingly, and whoever sows generously will also reap generously." This principle is not just a financial truth; it's a spiritual reality that reflects the heart of God. When we invest in the Kingdom, we're aligning ourselves with God's generous nature and His desire to bless and prosper His people — not just individually, but collectively.

Our willingness to invest financially in Kingdom initiatives goes beyond the act of giving. It is an acknowledgement of our stewardship over the resources God has entrusted to us. We are reminded in 1 Chronicles 29:14, as King David acknowledges during the temple offering, "Everything comes from you, and we have given you only what comes from your hand." This perspective transforms our giving from a duty to a joyful act of worship, recognizing that we are simply returning a portion of God's abundant blessings back into His work.

The impact of financial unity is multifaceted. Firstly, it furthers God's work on earth. Through our collective financial resources, churches and ministries can undertake projects, support missions, aid the needy, and create infrastructures that propagate the Gospel. Each contribution is a thread woven into the larger narrative of God's redemptive plan for humanity.

Moreover, our willingness to contribute financially strengthens the bonds within our community. It fosters a sense of ownership and shared purpose among members, as everyone plays a part in the Kingdom's advancement. This shared commitment brings a sense of unity and solidarity, as illustrated in the early church where believers "had everything in common" (Acts 2:44). This unity is not just in spirit but in practical, tangible actions that signify our mutual dedication to God's vision.

Financial giving is also an opportunity for spiritual growth. It challenges us to trust in God's provision, to prioritize Kingdom values over worldly gain, and to cultivate a heart of generosity — a heart that mirrors the heart of Christ. As Jesus himself said, "It is more blessed to give than to receive" (Acts 20:35). This act of giving enriches our spiritual lives, drawing us closer to God and to each other.

The willingness to sow and invest into the Kingdom financially is a crucial element of building a strong, resilient community in Christ. It is an expression of our faith, our trust in God's provision, and our commitment to the collective mission of the Church. As we give, we not only witness the growth and impact of our contributions in the tangible world but also experience a deepening of our spiritual connections and a strengthening of the communal bonds within the Body of Christ. Let this chapter be an invitation to embrace the joy of giving and to witness the abundant harvest that results from our collective investment in the Kingdom of God.

We Have Greater Success with Good Partners

In the realm of Kingdom Building, the journey towards fulfilling God's vision is often marked by the presence of allies and companions – partners who share the same heartbeat for the mission. Financial endeavors within the Kingdom echo this truth, shining a spotlight on the immense value of reliable and committed partners. This section of Chapter 6 navigates through the fertile plains of partnership, where shared values and goals weave together to create a synergy that amplifies the impact of our financial efforts.

Imagine a group of climbers, roped together as they ascend a steep mountain. Each climber brings their own strength, expertise, and resources, but it is their collective effort that ensures a safe and successful climb. In this imagery lies the essence of good partnership in financial endeavors. It's a unified movement, where each partner's contribution enhances the group's ability to reach new heights.

The Bible illuminates this concept beautifully in Ecclesiastes 4:9-10, "Two are better than one, because they have a good return for their labor: If either of them falls down, one can help the other up." This passage not only extols the virtues of companionship but also underscores the practical benefits of collaborative efforts. In the context of financial unity, this principle means that when we join forces with good partners, our collective resources and efforts yield a greater return than what we could achieve alone.

Good partners in financial endeavors are those who understand the significance of mutual support, shared responsibility, and collective vision. They are individuals or entities who are not only committed to contributing resources but are also dedicated to ensuring that these resources are used effectively and responsibly. Such partnerships are built on a foundation of trust, transparency, and a shared commitment to the Kingdom's values.

The impact of these partnerships is manifold. Firstly, they enhance the effectiveness of financial contributions. When resources are pooled together under a unified vision, they can be allocated more strategically, addressing needs more comprehensively and efficiently. For instance, a partnership among churches or ministries can lead to the establishment of larger community projects, such as building schools or hospitals, which would be challenging to accomplish single-handedly.

Furthermore, good partnerships extend the reach of our financial efforts. By combining resources and networks, we can impact a wider demographic, spreading the message of the Gospel farther and wider. This collaborative approach echoes the mission strategy seen in the New Testament, where Paul often partnered with other believers like Priscilla and Aquila to advance the Gospel (Acts 18:2-3).

Another vital aspect of successful partnerships is the shared experience of growth and learning. Partners challenge and sharpen one another, as Proverbs 27:17 states, "As iron sharpens iron, so one person sharpens another." This mutual edification not only strengthens the individual partners but also enriches the collective endeavor.

Financial success in Kingdom initiatives is significantly enhanced by the presence of good partners. These partnerships, rooted in shared values and goals, create a powerful synergy that maximizes the impact of our contributions. As we explore the concept of financial unity in this chapter, let us be encouraged to seek and nurture such partnerships. Let us remember that when we join hands with others who share our vision and commitment, we are not just pooling our resources; we are multiplying our impact, extending our reach, and collectively moving closer to fulfilling the great commission entrusted to us by Christ. Through these partnerships, we can truly witness the unfolding of God's work in remarkable ways, as we labor together in the vineyard of the Lord.

Be Honest with Those You Partner with About Your Portion of the Financial Contribution

"Be Honest with Those You Partner With About Your Portion of the Financial Contribution"

In the sacred journey of financial unity within the Kingdom, honesty and transparency are like the guiding stars that navigate the ship of partnership. They are essential virtues that maintain the trust and unity among partners. This chapter section invites us to explore the profound importance of being forthright about our financial contributions, a practice that not only prevents misunderstandings but also fosters a healthy environment where each person's commitment is respected and valued.

Imagine a group of builders, each tasked with bringing specific materials to construct a house. If one builder promises bricks but brings straw, the integrity of the entire structure is compromised. Similarly, in financial partnerships within the Kingdom, each member's contribution is like a vital building block in the edifice of God's work. Open communication about these contributions ensures that the structure of our collective mission is strong and resilient.

The biblical principle of honesty in dealings is clearly articulated in Proverbs 11:1, "The Lord detests dishonest scales, but accurate weights find favor with him." This scripture is a powerful reminder that God values integrity, especially in matters of stewardship and resources. In the context of financial partnerships, this translates to being transparent about our ability and commitment to contribute. It involves having open discussions and mutually agreeing upon the portion each partner can and will contribute.

Such honesty is crucial in preventing misunderstandings that can lead to discord. In Acts 5:1-11, the story of Ananias and Sapphira serves as a stark warning about the consequences of dishonesty in financial commitments within the Christian community. Their failure to be transparent about their contribution led to a tragic outcome, underscoring the importance of integrity in our dealings.

Openly discussing financial contributions also ensures that everyone is on the same page. It allows for effective planning and allocation of resources, ensuring that the collective effort is directed efficiently towards the Kingdom's goals. This clarity fosters a sense of collective responsibility and accountability, essential ingredients in a successful partnership.

Moreover, when each partner's financial commitment is respected and valued, it creates a culture of mutual respect and honor. This culture is crucial for maintaining a healthy and thriving partnership. It allows each member to feel valued and integral to the collective mission, irrespective of the size of their contribution. As stated in 2 Corinthians 8:12, "For if the willingness is there, the gift is acceptable according to what one has, not according to what one does not have." This scripture highlights that it is the heart behind the giving that matters most.

Being honest about financial contributions also builds trust among partners. Trust is the cornerstone of any healthy relationship, and in the context of financial partnerships, it is the glue that holds the collective vision together. When partners are honest and transparent with each other, it creates a foundation of trust that can withstand the challenges and obstacles that may arise.

Honesty and transparency about our financial contributions in the Kingdom's work are not optional virtues; they are indispensable. They ensure that our collective efforts are built on a foundation of integrity, mutual respect, and trust. As we navigate through the waters of financial unity, let us hold fast to these principles, remembering that our honesty in financial matters is a reflection of our commitment to the truth of the Gospel. In doing so, we not only strengthen our partnerships but also honor God, who is the ultimate source and steward of all our resources.

Come Together and Seek Out and Sow into Good Soil/Kingdom Soil

In Kingdom Building, the act of coming together to seek and sow into good soil is akin to a collective pilgrimage towards a fertile land, one that promises yield beyond mere temporal gains. This section of the chapter calls us to a journey of discernment and unity, where we, as a community, identify and invest in Kingdom initiatives — the 'good soil' that bears spiritual and communal fruit. It is an endeavor that goes beyond the act of giving; it is about strategically placing our resources where they can flourish and multiply, aligning with God's purposes and creating lasting, positive impacts.

Visualize a group of farmers gathering to discuss the best fields to plant their seeds. They examine the soil, discuss the climate, and share wisdom from past experiences. In this collaboration, they aim to find the most fertile ground that will ensure the best harvest. Similarly, in our financial endeavors for the Kingdom, we gather to discern where our resources can be most effective. This discernment process is not a solo expedition but a collective journey, underscored by prayer, wisdom, and guidance from the Holy Spirit.

The biblical parable of the sower (Matthew 13:3-9) serves as a profound metaphor for this process. The sower scatters seeds, some of which fall on good soil and yield a significant harvest. This parable teaches us about the importance of sowing into receptive ground — investments that align with God's purposes and have the potential for substantial spiritual and communal returns.

Identifying good soil requires a deep understanding of God's vision for His Kingdom. It calls for discernment — the ability to judge well. In Proverbs 3:5-6, we are encouraged to, "Trust in the Lord with all your heart and lean not on your own understanding; in all your ways submit to him, and he will make your paths straight." This scripture highlights the importance of seeking divine guidance in our decision-making processes.

Collective decision-making ensures that financial resources are allocated effectively and responsibly. It involves engaging in meaningful dialogue, sharing insights, and respecting diverse viewpoints, ultimately leading to a consensus on where to sow our resources. By investing collectively in good soil, we not only maximize the impact of our resources but also strengthen our unity as a community of believers.

Sowing into good soil means supporting projects and missions that resonate with God's heart. These could range from local community outreach programs to international missions, from church planting initiatives to humanitarian aid efforts. Each investment is a testament to our faith and commitment to God's command to love and serve others.

Coming together to seek and sow into good soil is a critical aspect of financial unity in the Kingdom of God. It is an exercise in spiritual discernment, collective wisdom, and strategic investment. As we undertake this journey, let us be guided by prayer, united in purpose, and committed to sowing our resources into fertile grounds where they can yield a hundredfold. In doing so, we honor God's provisions and play our part in the unfolding story of His Kingdom on earth.

Keep the Goal Before You

In the journey of Kingdom Building, particularly in the realm of financial unity, it's crucial to maintain a steadfast gaze on the ultimate goal – the advancement of God's Kingdom. This chapter section beckons us to embrace a perspective that transcends mere monetary achievements, focusing instead on the grand vision of spreading the Gospel, nurturing communities, and transforming lives.

Envision yourself as an archer, aiming at a target in the distance. The wind may blow, distractions may arise, but your eyes remain fixed on the bullseye. In the same manner, in our financial endeavors for the Kingdom, challenges and delays are inevitable, but our focus must remain unshaken – fixed on the goal of God's Kingdom advancement.

The biblical narrative of Nehemiah rebuilding the walls of Jerusalem serves as a powerful allegory for this unwavering focus. Faced with opposition and discouragement, Nehemiah kept his purpose at the forefront: to restore and fortify the city for the glory of God (Nehemiah 6:3). His story teaches us that keeping our goal in sight is crucial for overcoming obstacles and staying true to our mission.

Philippians 3:14 encapsulates this sentiment: "I press on toward the goal to win the prize for which God has called me heavenward in Christ Jesus." Like Paul, we are called to press on toward our goal, not swayed by temporary setbacks or enticed by superficial gains. Our aim is not just financial prosperity but the prosperity of the Kingdom – a realm where the Gospel flourishes, lives are transformed, and communities are uplifted.

Keeping the goal before us ensures that our financial contributions and efforts are aligned with the broader vision of God's work. It inspires commitment and perseverance, motivating us to contribute not out of obligation but out of a desire to see the Kingdom grow and thrive.

As we navigate the complexities and responsibilities of financial unity in the Kingdom, let us continually keep the goal before us. Let this goal be the beacon that guides our decisions, the anchor that holds us steady in times of uncertainty, and the inspiration that fuels our passion and commitment. Our ultimate aim is not merely financial gain but the advancement of God's Kingdom, the spreading of the Gospel, and the betterment of communities and lives. In this pursuit, every financial decision becomes an act of worship, an offering towards a grander, divine purpose.

Pray for a Great Harvest

In the sacred act of financial unity and giving within the Kingdom, prayer emerges as a pivotal element, a divine conduit through which our efforts and hopes ascend to God, seeking His blessing and guidance. This section of the chapter draws us into the profound realm of prayer, emphasizing its critical role in anticipating and seeking a great harvest from our financial sowing.

Visualize a gardener who, after planting seeds, kneels beside the garden bed, hands folded, and heart open, whispering prayers for a bountiful harvest. This image is a poignant reflection of our stance in financial unity. We plant seeds in the form of financial contributions, and then we turn to prayer, entrusting God with the growth and fruition of these seeds.

The biblical principle of seeking God's intervention and blessing in our endeavors is beautifully captured in James 5:16, "The prayer of a righteous person is powerful and effective." Through prayer, we align our financial sowing with God's will, inviting His omnipotent hand to work in and through our contributions. It's an acknowledgment that while we can plant and water, it is God who brings the growth (1 Corinthians 3:6-7).

Praying for a great harvest is not merely a request for multiplied resources; it is a deeper plea for God to use our contributions for His glory and the expansion of His Kingdom. It is a prayer that the funds we sow will bear fruit in the form of changed lives, strengthened communities, and the spread of the Gospel.

Moreover, such prayer encompasses a request for blessings upon the endeavors and people that these financial seeds support. It is an intercession for guidance, wisdom, and success for the missions, projects, and individuals involved, echoing the sentiment in Philippians 4:19, where Paul assures that "my God will meet all your needs according to the riches of his glory in Christ Jesus."

In conclusion, as we engage in the sacred practice of financial unity, let prayer be our constant companion. Let us earnestly seek God's blessing and guidance, praying for a great harvest that extends beyond mere monetary gain, reaching into the realms of spiritual growth, Kingdom advancement, and the betterment of lives. In this way, our financial sowing becomes intertwined with spiritual longing, creating a powerful synergy that transcends human effort and enters the realm of divine possibility.

It Takes Two to Build and Two Is Better Than One

There lies a simple yet profound truth: it takes two to build, and indeed, two is better than one. This section of the chapter invites us into the realm of collaborative effort, where the power of partnership is celebrated as a cornerstone in the edifice of God's work.

Envision two musicians, each skilled in their own right, coming together to create a harmony that neither could achieve alone. Their individual notes, when played in concert, create a melody that resonates with a richness and depth unattainable in solitude. Similarly, in the context of Kingdom Building, the collaboration between individuals amplifies the impact and scope of the work undertaken.

The biblical wisdom in Ecclesiastes 4:9-10 eloquently captures this concept: "Two are better than one, because they have a good return for their labor: If either of them falls down, one can help the other up." This scripture is not merely a testament to the practical benefits of working together but also a reflection of the spiritual and emotional support inherent in partnerships.

In the journey of building God's Kingdom, whether in financial undertakings, ministry work, or community service, the partnership between individuals is invaluable. Each person brings unique strengths, perspectives, and resources to the table. When these are combined, the potential for success and impact is greatly multiplied.

Moreover, the partnership is not just about combining resources; it's about sharing the journey, the challenges, and the triumphs. In moments of difficulty, having a partner offers encouragement and support, reinforcing the resolve to persevere. In times of success, it provides someone to share in the joy and to give thanks to God with.

Let us embrace the wisdom of collaboration. It takes two to build, and truly, two is better than one. By joining hands with others, we can create something far greater than what we can achieve alone. In this unity of purpose and effort, we reflect the very nature of the Church, a body of believers, working together in harmony for the fulfillment of God's grand design.

As we reach the conclusion of Chapter 6, we recognize that financial unity in the Kingdom of God transcends the mere aggregation of resources. It represents a profound act of faith and commitment, a testament to our collective endeavor to advance God's Kingdom on Earth. This unity is not just about the funds we pool together; it is about the spiritual connections we fortify and the shared vision we nurture. Through our collaborative financial efforts, we contribute to a larger narrative of hope, transformation, and growth. Each contribution, big or small, is a vital thread in the larger fabric of God's work. As we move forward, let us carry with us the understanding that in our unity, there is strength — a strength that not only supports the physical needs of the Church and its mission but also bolsters our spiritual resolve and deepens our communal bonds in Christ.

Chapter 7

God's Purpose in Relationships

As we journey into Chapter 7, "God's Purpose in Relationships," we embark on a deeper exploration into the spiritual dimension of our interactions and connections. This chapter is a profound reflection on how our relationships are not just earthly ties but are, in essence, designed to be conduits for spiritual growth and catalysts for Kingdom impact. It's an invitation to align our relational dynamics with God's divine purpose, seeing beyond the superficial to grasp the eternal significance woven into our connections.

The fabric of our relationships is intricately designed by God, each thread purposed to strengthen, encourage, and challenge us in our faith journey. Relationships in the Kingdom are far more than mere social interactions; they are opportunities for spiritual edification and expressions of God's love. As we delve into this chapter, we uncover the biblical perspective on relationships, recognizing them as platforms for demonstrating Christ-like love, grace, and forgiveness.

We explore how relationships serve as mirrors, reflecting our own spiritual state and prompting us to grow in Christlikeness. In our interactions with others, we are often faced with scenarios that test our patience, kindness, and humility, pushing us to develop the fruits of the Spirit as outlined in Galatians 5:22-23. Our connections become a training ground for spiritual development, where virtues are honed and character is shaped.

Furthermore, this chapter highlights how God uses relationships to fulfill His larger purpose — the spreading of the Gospel and the building of His Kingdom. Our relationships are channels through which God's love and truth flow, impacting lives and drawing others closer to Him. They are the threads in the larger tapestry of God's redemptive plan, each connection interwoven to form the beautiful picture of the Church in unity and purpose.

Chapter 7 brings to the forefront the profound realization that every relationship is imbued with a divine purpose. It encourages readers to view their connections through the lens of eternity, recognizing the potential each one holds for spiritual growth, Kingdom impact, and the fulfillment of God's overarching plan. As we navigate our relationships, let us do so with intentionality and a heart attuned to God's purposes, transforming our everyday interactions into eternal investments.

You Will Go Through Spiritual Warfare When Kingdom Building

In the sacred journey of Kingdom Building, there lies a stark yet empowering truth: the path is often intersected by spiritual warfare. This section of Chapter 7 delves into the heart of this reality, acknowledging that as we engage in God's work, our challenges are not merely physical or emotional, but deeply spiritual. This dimension of spiritual warfare, though daunting, serves as a crucible for our faith, strengthening our relationships and fortifying our resolve in the mission.

Picture a group of ancient warriors, not just armed with physical weapons but also fortified with a deep understanding of their cause and unwavering determination. Similarly, in our spiritual journey, we are called to arm ourselves with the full armor of God, as described in Ephesians 6:10-18. The apostle Paul's vivid imagery of spiritual armor — including the belt of truth, the breastplate of righteousness, and the sword of the Spirit — is not just symbolic but a directive for our spiritual readiness.

Engaging in Kingdom Building is a noble yet challenging endeavor. As John Maxwell aptly stated, "The greatest day in your life and mine is when we take total responsibility for our attitudes. That's the day we truly grow up." This responsibility extends to recognizing that our spiritual attitudes determine our resilience in spiritual battles. Opposition and challenges, whether in the form of discouragement, conflict, or temptation, are often heightened when we commit to living out God's purpose in our relationships and endeavors.

This warfare is not an indication of defeat or abandonment; rather, it's a testament to the significance of the work we are undertaking. The enemy's resistance is often strongest when we are closest to achieving a breakthrough for the Kingdom. Just as gold is refined by fire, our faith and relationships are purified and strengthened through these spiritual battles. In James 1:2-4, we are reminded to consider it pure joy when we face trials of many kinds, because the testing of our faith produces perseverance.

Understanding and embracing God's purpose in our relationships is crucial in navigating these spiritual battles. When we perceive our connections as avenues for God's work, we become more vigilant, supportive, and united in our efforts. Our relationships transform into partnerships in the battle, marked by mutual encouragement, prayer, and support.

Furthermore, the warfare we encounter can deepen our connections with others. Shared struggles often lead to strengthened bonds. As we support one another, pray for one another, and stand together in faith, our unity in Christ is solidified. This unity is our greatest strength in spiritual warfare, as Jesus himself prayed for his disciples, "that they may be one as we are one" (John 17:11).

Recognizing and preparing for spiritual warfare is integral to Kingdom Building. This chapter is not just a call to awareness but an invitation to arm ourselves with faith, truth, and unity. As we navigate these spiritual battles, our relationships become more than just social connections; they transform into divine alliances, fortifying our resolve and deepening our impact for the Kingdom. Let us, therefore, embrace this journey with courage and faith, holding onto the promise that "He who is in you is greater than he who is in the world" (1 John 4:4). In this knowledge, we find the strength to overcome and the hope to persevere, as we continue to build God's Kingdom together.

Make Time to Meditate on The Word of God with Your Partner

In the pursuit of building relationships grounded in faith and purpose, one of the most profound practices is the shared meditation on the Word of God. This section of Chapter 7 explores the enriching journey of diving into Scripture alongside your partner, a journey that not only fosters individual spiritual growth but also cements your bond in mutual understanding, faith, and a shared vision aligned with God's will.

Picture a serene morning, where two souls sit together, Bibles open, hearts open even wider, ready to receive and reflect on the divine wisdom contained within the Scriptures. This image encapsulates the beauty of meditating on God's Word with your partner. It's a sacred time set apart from the bustle of life, a time where the noise of the world fades and the voice of God takes precedence.

The Bible, in Joshua 1:8, advises, "Keep this Book of the Law always on your lips; meditate on it day and night, so that you may be careful to do everything written in it. Then you will be prosperous and successful." This scripture is not merely a call to individual meditation but an invitation to couples to collectively immerse themselves in God's teachings. In doing so, they allow His Word to guide, shape, and mold their relationship.

This practice of shared meditation is a journey through the treasures of wisdom, instruction, and encouragement found in the Bible. It involves reading, studying, and discussing the Scriptures together, thereby allowing God's truth to seep into every aspect of the relationship. As each partner shares insights and revelations, they not only gain a deeper understanding of the Word but also of each other. This mutual exploration leads to a synchrony of faith and values, strengthening the bond between them.

Furthermore, meditating on the Word together lays a foundation for a relationship that is aligned with God's purposes. As couples navigate through life's challenges and joys, the Scriptures serve as a compass, pointing them towards Godly responses and decisions. In times of conflict or decision-making, the Word offers guidance and wisdom, as mentioned in Psalm 119:105, "Your word is a lamp for my feet, a light on my path." It becomes the anchor that holds the relationship steady amidst the storms of life.

Moreover, this shared spiritual discipline opens channels of communication that transcend the ordinary. Discussions about Scripture can lead to profound conversations about life, purpose, and faith, fostering a deeper emotional and spiritual intimacy. It's an opportunity to pray together, seeking God's will for the relationship and for each other, as exemplified in Matthew 18:19, "Again, truly I tell you that if two of you on earth agree about anything they ask for, it will be done for them by my Father in heaven."

Making time to meditate on the Word of God with your partner is a powerful way to strengthen your relationship. It is an act that goes beyond individual spiritual growth, bonding partners together in a shared journey of faith. This practice not only aligns the relationship with God's will but also enriches it with deeper understanding, mutual respect, and a united purpose. As couples commit to this practice, they build a relationship that is not just rooted in love for each other but also anchored in a profound love for God and His Word.

There is Power in Prayer When Two or More Like-Minded People Come Together

In the sacred landscape of Kingdom Building, prayer stands as a towering beacon of hope and power. Particularly, when two or more like-minded individuals unite in prayer, they tap into a profound spiritual synergy that transcends human understanding. This section of Chapter 7 delves into the remarkable power of united prayer, exploring how this shared spiritual discipline invites God's presence and power into relationships, fostering breakthroughs, guidance, and a strengthened faith.

Imagine a scene where two travelers, journeying through a dense forest, suddenly find themselves at a crossroads. Unsure of the path to take, they pause and join hands, their voices uniting in prayer, seeking divine guidance. In this moment of united prayer, there's a palpable shift — a sense of peace and clarity descends upon them. This imagery captures the essence of the power that manifests when like-minded believers come together in prayer.

The Bible offers profound insight into this power. Matthew 18:19-20 declares, "Again I say to you, if two of you agree on earth about anything they ask, it will be done for them by my Father in heaven. For where two or three are gathered in my name, there am I among them." These words of Jesus highlight not just the effectiveness of united prayer, but also the promise of His presence in such gatherings. When believers join in prayer, they create a space for God to move, for His will to unfold, and for His power to be unleashed in their lives and circumstances.

United prayer, especially within the context of relationships, is more than a ritual; it's a powerful act of faith. When couples, friends, or family members come together in prayer, they align their hearts, hopes, and desires with God's will. They stand as witnesses to each other's petitions, offering support, encouragement, and affirmation. This act of unity in prayer fosters a spiritual bond that is resilient and enduring.

Furthermore, this collective prayer often leads to breakthroughs — moments of divine intervention and revelation. It's in these moments of joint supplication that barriers are broken, obstacles are overcome, and answers are received. The early church, as described in Acts, frequently gathered for united prayer, and they witnessed remarkable outcomes, from Peter's miraculous release from prison to the outpouring of the Holy Spirit at Pentecost.

United prayer also brings guidance and direction in relationships. When decisions are to be made or paths are to be chosen, praying together invites divine wisdom and discernment. As Proverbs 3:5-6 advises, "Trust in the Lord with all your heart, and lean not on your own understanding; in all your ways submit to him, and he will make your paths straight." Prayer becomes the means through which God's guidance is sought and received.

Moreover, praying together strengthens faith. It serves as a reminder of God's faithfulness and power. Each answered prayer, each moment of divine presence, fortifies the belief in God's goodness and His active role in our lives. This shared experience of witnessing God's hand at work strengthens not just individual faith but the collective faith of those praying together.

In conclusion, the power of united prayer in the lives of like-minded believers is immense and immeasurable. As we explore this truth in Chapter 7, let us be encouraged to seek out and cherish these moments of joint prayer. Let us remember that when we come together in prayer, we open the doors to God's miraculous works, we invite His guidance and wisdom, and we strengthen the bonds of faith and fellowship. In this unity of prayer, there is indeed power — power to transform, to guide, and to sustain.

When One Partner Deals with Adversity, the Other Partner Can Fill In

The journey of any relationship is often interspersed with seasons of adversity. It is during these challenging periods that the depth, resilience, and true strength of the partnership are most powerfully displayed. This section of Chapter 7 is a poignant exploration of how, in times of difficulty, one partner's strength becomes the other's sanctuary, how the love and commitment shared between two people shine brightest in the moments of supporting and uplifting each other.

Consider the story of a couple, where one partner, unexpectedly, faces a health crisis. The vibrant rhythm of their life is disrupted, and the sick partner finds themselves wrestling not just with physical pain but also with the emotional turmoil of feeling like a burden. The other partner, witnessing this struggle, becomes a pillar of strength — not just taking on additional responsibilities but also offering constant emotional support and encouragement. Their actions become the living embodiment of the biblical injunction in Galatians 6:2, "Carry each other's burdens, and in this way you will fulfill the law of Christ."

This sacrificial gesture of stepping in, of filling the gaps left by adversity, is a testament to the unconditional love and commitment that form the bedrock of a strong relationship. It's a reflection of the selfless love Christ exemplified and called us to emulate. In these moments, the partnership transcends the realm of mere companionship and enters a sacred space of shared suffering and mutual support.

The resilience built through such experiences is invaluable. As one partner battles adversity, the other's support mitigates the feelings of isolation and despair that often accompany difficult times. This solidarity in the face of trials not only fortifies the individual facing adversity but also deepens the bond between the partners. It is a powerful reminder of the Scripture in Ecclesiastes 4:10, "If either of them falls down, one can help the other up. But pity anyone who falls and has no one to help them up."

Furthermore, these moments of filling in for one another are not limited to grand gestures or monumental sacrifices. Often, it is the small, daily acts of kindness and understanding — a reassuring word, a listening ear, or a comforting embrace — that weave a stronger fabric of connection. These acts of love and support are a practical demonstration of 1 John 3:18, "Let us not love with words or speech but with actions and in truth."

In such times, prayer becomes a vital tool. The partner not facing adversity can intercede on behalf of the other, seeking strength, healing, and comfort from God. This intercession is a powerful act of love, an expression of faith and trust in God's providence and care.

The role one plays in stepping in for a partner dealing with adversity is a crucial aspect of a healthy, God-centered relationship. It is a demonstration of the 'agape' love — a selfless, sacrificial love that seeks the well-being of the other. These moments of adversity, while challenging, are opportunities to manifest the depth of commitment and love that exists within the relationship. They are a testament to the resilience that can be built when two individuals commit to supporting each other, no matter the circumstance, echoing the enduring promise and hope found in God's Word.

Always Be Willing to Encourage and Uplift

In the dance of relationships, the steps of encouragement and upliftment play a pivotal role. These actions are the gentle wind beneath the wings of partnerships, especially in the journey of Kingdom Building, where the path is often strewn with challenges and trials. The continuous commitment to encourage and support one another is not just a virtue; it's a vital element that infuses strength, hope, and resilience into the relationship.

In a quaint town, there lived a couple known for their devotion to community service and their unwavering faith. Despite their tireless work, they occasionally faced setbacks and criticism that dampened their spirits. During these times, they found solace and strength in each other's encouragement. The husband, when seeing his wife disheartened, would gently remind her of her invaluable impact, quoting Philippians 4:13, "I can do all things through Christ who strengthens me." These words were not mere utterances but a powerful affirmation of her capabilities and God's unwavering support.

Similarly, the wife, in moments when her husband felt overwhelmed by the weight of their mission, would uplift him with words of encouragement, often reflecting on Proverbs 3:5-6, "Trust in the Lord with all your heart and lean not on your own understanding; in all your ways submit to him, and he will make your paths straight." Her encouragement served as a beacon of light, guiding him back to the path of trust and perseverance.

Their story exemplifies the profound impact of continuous encouragement and support in a relationship. It highlights how positive reinforcement, rooted in faith and love, creates a nurturing environment that fosters growth, both individually and collectively. Their commitment to uplifting each other was not a mere response to challenging times; it was a habitual practice, ingrained in their daily interactions.

This practice of mutual encouragement is not only essential in overcoming external challenges but also in navigating internal struggles. Each partner, in their moments of self-doubt or weakness, finds a reservoir of strength in the other's uplifting words and actions. This interchange of support and encouragement becomes a testament to their love, echoing the words of 1 Thessalonians 5:11, "Therefore encourage one another and build each other up, just as in fact you are doing."

Furthermore, the act of encouraging and uplifting each other extends beyond the confines of the relationship and impacts the community around them. A couple or partnership fortified with encouragement becomes a source of inspiration and hope for others. Their relationship becomes a reflection of God's love and grace, a beacon that illuminates the path for others in their spiritual journey.

In the realm of Kingdom Building, where the work can be daunting and the obstacles many, the importance of having a partner who embodies the spirit of encouragement cannot be overstated. Their words of affirmation, acts of kindness, and unwavering support act as a lifeline, sustaining and empowering one another to continue the noble task they have embarked upon.

The willingness to continuously encourage and uplift each other is a golden thread in the fabric of a strong, resilient relationship. It is a commitment that breathes life and vitality into the partnership, enabling both individuals to face challenges with courage and to embrace their journey with hope. This practice of mutual encouragement and support, grounded in the wisdom of the Scriptures, not only deepens the connection between partners but also aligns them more closely with God's purpose and mission. As they walk hand in hand, lifting each other up, they embody the very essence of a Christ-centered relationship, radiating love, hope, and strength to each other and to the world around them.

Be Quick to Forgive One Another

In the journey of building relationships, especially within the realm of Kingdom Building, forgiveness emerges not just as an act of grace, but as an essential element for the survival and flourishing of any partnership. This section of Chapter 7 sheds light on the profound importance of being swift to forgive, understanding that the absence of forgiveness is often the breeding ground for bitterness and resentment, which can severely undermine the unity and health of a relationship.

The story of a seasoned missionary couple, Sarah and John, serves as a poignant example of this principle. Their journey in spreading the Gospel was not without its share of challenges and conflicts. On one occasion, in the midst of a heated discussion over their ministry's direction, harsh words were exchanged, leaving both feeling wounded and misunderstood. However, instead of allowing these hurts to fester, Sarah and John turned to the wisdom of Ephesians 4:32, "Be kind and compassionate to one another, forgiving each other, just as in Christ God forgave you." Remembering this, they made the conscious decision to address the issue openly, extend forgiveness, and move forward.

Their decision to forgive was not a sign of weakness or an act of mere obligation. It was a powerful demonstration of their commitment to the teachings of Christ and their understanding of the imperatives of Kingdom work. They recognized that harboring unforgiveness not only impacted their relationship but also hindered their ministry. Forgiveness became a pathway to reconciliation and deeper understanding.

Forgiveness in relationships, especially in the context of spiritual warfare and Kingdom Building, is vital in maintaining the armor of God. Unforgiveness is akin to a chink in this armor, through which the enemy can infiltrate and cause disruption. In Matthew 6:14-15, Jesus underscores the importance of forgiveness, linking it to our own forgiveness by God: "For if you forgive other people when they sin against you, your heavenly Father will also forgive you. But if you do not forgive others their sins, your Father will not forgive your sins." This statement is a solemn reminder of the weight and necessity of forgiveness in our spiritual and relational lives.

Forgiveness also plays a critical role in preserving unity within relationships. In the case of Sarah and John, their ability to forgive each other was instrumental in maintaining the strength and focus of their partnership. It allowed them to overcome barriers, heal from wounds, and continue their mission with renewed vigor and unity.

Moreover, forgiveness opens the door for God's healing and restoration to flow into relationships. It transforms potential areas of weakness into testimonies of God's grace and mercy. In moments where forgiveness is extended, relationships are not just mended; they are often strengthened, bearing witness to the redemptive power of Christ's love.

The practice of being quick to forgive is a cornerstone in the foundation of any healthy, Christ-centered relationship. It is an act that goes beyond the resolution of conflicts; it is a commitment to emulate the forgiveness we have received in Christ. As we navigate through the complexities of relationships, let us be guided by the principle of swift forgiveness, ensuring that our connections are marked by grace, love, and unity. In doing so, we not only maintain the health and vitality of our relationships but also uphold the principles of the Kingdom we strive to build.

One Can Chase a Thousand Evil Spirits Away but Two Spirit Filled People Can Put 10,000 Demons to Flight

In the vast expanse of spiritual warfare, there lies a powerful truth about the amplified strength that emerges when two Spirit-filled individuals unite in purpose and faith. This section of Chapter 7 delves deep into the biblical principle that emphasizes the magnified impact of united partners in the face of spiritual battles. It's an exploration of how relationships, when grounded in God and His purpose, transform into formidable weapons against the forces of darkness, enabling couples or partners to confront and overcome monumental adversities for the Kingdom of God.

The story of David and Jonathan in the Scriptures provides a stirring example of this truth. Though not facing literal demons, their united front against the adversities of life showcases the principle vividly. Jonathan, the son of King Saul, and David, a humble shepherd who would become king, forged a bond grounded in faith and mutual respect. When Jonathan recognized the anointing on David, he didn't allow jealousy or fear to dictate his actions. Instead, he chose to stand with David, even when it meant opposing his father, Saul. Their partnership was not just a testament to their friendship but also to their shared commitment to God's plan. In their unity, they displayed formidable strength – a strength that echoes the promise found in Deuteronomy 32:30, "How could one man chase a thousand, or two put ten thousand to flight, unless their Rock had sold them, unless the Lord had given them up?"

This biblical principle is not just a metaphor for physical battles; it is a profound truth in spiritual warfare. When two Spirit-filled individuals come together, their combined spiritual authority exponentially increases. They become a force to be reckoned with, capable of overcoming greater challenges and achieving more significant victories for the Kingdom. Their united prayer, faith, and action have the power to shift atmospheres, break chains of bondage, and usher in God's presence and power.

In modern times, consider a couple deeply involved in ministry, facing opposition and spiritual attacks. Individually, they each have strengths and a deep faith. However, when they come together in prayer and action, their combined spiritual authority escalates. In moments of joint prayer, they are not just two individuals; they become a united front, embodying the Scripture from Matthew 18:19-20, "Again, truly I tell you that if two of you on earth agree about anything they ask for, it will be done for them by my Father in heaven. For where two or three gather in my name, there am I with them." Their united stand in faith and prayer becomes a powerful conduit for God's intervention, turning the tide in spiritual battles and bringing victory where there once seemed none.

Furthermore, this unity and shared purpose in relationships do more than just deepen connections; they enable individuals to fulfill their God-given destinies more effectively. When partners support, pray for, and stand with each other, they unlock potential and purposes in each other that might have remained dormant. Their combined strengths and gifts, under the guidance of the Holy Spirit, lead them to accomplish far more than they could have separately.

The principle that one can chase a thousand, but two can put ten thousand to flight, is a stirring reminder of the power of unity in spiritual warfare. As we embrace God's purpose in our relationships, we transform them into potent instruments for Kingdom Building. These partnerships, forged and fueled by the Spirit, enable us to confront and conquer formidable challenges, achieving victories that resonate far beyond our individual capacities. In this divine synergy, we not only find strength and victory but also fulfill our destinies in Christ, advancing His Kingdom together.

As we draw Chapter 7 to a close, we reflect on the transformative journey of our relationships under the sovereign hand of God. This chapter has illuminated how, by aligning ourselves and our partnerships with His divine purpose, our relationships transcend mere human connections. They become powerful instruments in the hands of God, tools shaped and used for the monumental task of Kingdom Building. The ordinary is infused with the extraordinary, as each bond of friendship, marriage, or fellowship is reoriented towards a higher calling.

In this alignment with God's purpose, there's an unlocking of immense potential – potential for profound spiritual growth, for deeper connections, and for a more significant impact in the world around us. Our relationships, rooted in Christ and nurtured through faith, become sources of strength, encouragement, and resilience. They transform into havens of support in times of trial, incubators of growth in times of peace, and launchpads for action in times of opportunity.

As we navigate through the complexities of life, these God-centered relationships guide us, challenge us, and inspire us. They remind us that we are not solitary warriors in the spiritual battlefield, but part of a formidable army, united in purpose and spirit. The adversities and victories we encounter are not just individual experiences but shared chapters in the larger story of God's redemptive plan.

Our journey through this chapter calls us to view our relationships through the lens of eternity. It beckons us to invest in these divine connections, nurturing them with prayer, scripture, forgiveness, and unconditional love. As we do so, we become co-laborers with Christ, building His Kingdom one relationship at a time. The potential within each relationship is immense, and when harnessed for God's purposes, the impact is eternal. Let us, therefore, go forth with a renewed commitment to see our relationships not just as part of our earthly journey, but as integral to our heavenly calling.

Chapter 8

Navigating Challenges Together

In Chapter 8, "Navigating Challenges Together," we embark on a profound exploration of facing and overcoming the myriad challenges that arise in relationships. This journey is not about avoiding storms but learning to navigate through them with resilience, wisdom, and grace. The chapter unfolds the art of transforming obstacles into opportunities for growth, unity, and deeper connection. It is a guide to cultivating a fortress of support and understanding, essential for any relationship to not just survive but thrive amidst adversities.

Every relationship, no matter how strong or harmoniously it begins, will inevitably encounter its share of challenges. These can range from minor misunderstandings to major conflicts, from personal struggles to external pressures. However, it is not the presence of these challenges that defines a relationship, but the manner in which they are confronted and resolved. This chapter delves into practical strategies that equip couples, friends, and partners to face difficulties head-on, anchored in mutual support and understanding.

Central to navigating these challenges is the concept of unity. Unity does not imply a lack of conflict but represents a commitment to work through differences and difficulties together. It involves harnessing the strength found in collective resilience, where two or more people, bound by common purpose and love, become stronger than the sum of their parts. The chapter draws upon biblical wisdom and real-life examples to illustrate how unity, coupled with open communication, empathy, and patience, becomes an unbreakable cord that holds relationships together in the face of trials.

Moreover, this chapter addresses the importance of maintaining a spiritual foundation in relationships. It underscores how shared faith and reliance on God's guidance provide not just solace but also the strength to overcome challenges. Prayer, meditation on Scriptures, and spiritual support are explored as vital tools in fortifying relationships against the onslaught of life's storms.

"Navigating Challenges Together" is more than a chapter; it's a roadmap to building and sustaining robust relationships in a world fraught with challenges. It's about recognizing that the true strength of a relationship lies in how effectively challenges are navigated through collective resilience, unwavering support, and a shared commitment to grow and emerge stronger on the other side. As readers journey through this chapter, they will gain insights and tools to fortify their relationships, turning every challenge into a stepping stone towards a more profound, fulfilling partnership.

True Partnership is Not 50/50

The concept of true partnership often misleads many into striving for a 50/50 balance. However, as we delve into this crucial section of Chapter 8, we uncover a richer, more profound understanding of partnership, especially in the context of Kingdom Building. True partnership, we learn, transcends the idea of equal division; it is rooted in mutual support, understanding, and the shared journey of growth. It's about adapting, sharing burdens, and enhancing each other's strengths in a way that is flexible and responsive to each partner's needs at any given time.

The story of Mara and Liam, a couple deeply involved in ministry work, brings this principle to life. Mara, a vibrant and gifted speaker, often found herself at the forefront of their ministry endeavors, while Liam worked tirelessly behind the scenes, managing logistics and offering emotional support. Their partnership did not fit into the neat confines of a 50/50 division; instead, it fluidly adapted to the demands of each situation. When Liam's father fell ill, Mara took on more responsibilities in their ministry, allowing Liam to care for his family. In this season of their lives, the balance shifted, but so did their support for each other.

This fluidity in partnership echoes the Biblical principle found in Galatians 6:2, "Carry each other's burdens, and in this way, you will fulfill the law of Christ." The scripture emphasizes the call to support one another, understanding that at times, one partner may carry more weight than the other. This support is not about keeping score but about loving and serving one another in response to Christ's love for us.

True partnership also involves a deep level of understanding and empathy. It recognizes that each partner brings different strengths, weaknesses, and perspectives to the relationship. In 1 Corinthians 12:12-26, Paul describes the church as one body with many parts, each with a unique function. Similarly, in a partnership, each individual's unique contributions and capabilities are valued and considered essential to the health and function of the relationship.

Furthermore, this approach to partnership fosters growth and strength in the relationship. By sharing burdens and leaning on each other's strengths, partners not only navigate challenges more effectively but also experience personal and spiritual growth. This growth is beautifully depicted in the story of Ruth and Naomi, where Ruth's commitment to Naomi (Ruth 1:16-17) exemplifies a deep, selfless partnership. Their relationship, though not equal in the conventional sense, was profoundly impactful, leading to blessings that extended beyond their individual lives.

Moreover, a true partnership is built on the foundation of grace and forgiveness. Understanding that each partner is human and fallible, forgiveness becomes a crucial component in maintaining harmony and resilience in the relationship. Ephesians 4:32 encourages believers to "be kind and compassionate to one another, forgiving each other, just as in Christ God forgave you." This scripture not only urges forgiveness but also reminds us of the grace we have received, which we are to extend in our relationships.

True partnership in relationships, especially those rooted in Kingdom Building, is not about maintaining a rigid 50/50 balance. It is about a dynamic, responsive, and selfless commitment to support, understand, and grow with each other. It's about recognizing the varying needs and strengths within the relationship and adapting accordingly. As we journey through this section, we are reminded that the strength of a partnership lies not in equality of contribution but in the depth of commitment, the willingness to share burdens, and the capacity to enhance each other's strengths, all underpinned by a foundation of love, grace, and mutual respect.

Admit Your Shortcomings

In the intricate journey of relationships, especially those purposed for Kingdom building, the ability to admit one's shortcomings plays a pivotal role. It's a step that requires immense courage and humility, yet it is fundamental in paving the way for genuine communication, mutual growth, and deeper understanding. This section of Chapter 8 delves into the transformative power of acknowledging our flaws and mistakes, illustrating that this admission is not a sign of weakness, but rather a hallmark of strength and maturity.

In a small, close-knit community church, there was a couple, Ethan and Rachel, known for their dedication and service. However, like any relationship, theirs was not devoid of challenges. Ethan, though a devoted husband and a respected leader, struggled with impatience, often leading to unnecessary conflicts at home and within their ministry. Rachel, on the other hand, had a tendency to avoid confrontations, which sometimes resulted in unresolved issues. Their turning point came when Ethan, during a particularly tense disagreement, took a moment to reflect and then admitted his impatience to Rachel. This act of humility was based on the wisdom found in James 5:16, "Therefore confess your sins to each other and pray for each other so that you may be healed. The prayer of a righteous person is powerful and effective."

Ethan's admission was a powerful catalyst for change in their relationship. It opened the door for Rachel to express her feelings about their conflicts without fear of escalation. This mutual vulnerability led to a profound shift in their communication, fostering an environment of honesty and growth. Rachel, encouraged by Ethan's example, began to address her tendency to avoid difficult conversations, admitting her shortcomings and expressing her desire to change.

This dynamic change in their relationship not only improved their personal life but also positively impacted their ministry. Their congregation witnessed a tangible difference in their leadership – a newfound grace and patience that spoke volumes of their personal growth. This change was a living testament to the scripture in Proverbs 28:13, "Whoever conceals their sins does not prosper, but the one who confesses and renounces them finds mercy."

Moreover, Ethan and Rachel's journey highlighted that admitting shortcomings was not just about acknowledging faults; it was about taking proactive steps towards improvement and healing. It involved seeking forgiveness, extending grace, and actively working on personal growth, underpinned by prayer and reliance on God's strength.

Their story demonstrates that admitting one's shortcomings in a relationship is a profound act of love and respect for the other person. It shows a commitment to the health and growth of the relationship and acknowledges that personal transformation is an integral part of relational harmony.

The willingness to admit personal shortcomings is a crucial step in navigating challenges together. It demonstrates humility, strengthens communication, and fosters an environment conducive to mutual growth and deeper understanding. This admission is a testament to the strength and maturity of individuals who are dedicated to not just maintaining but enriching their relationships. As we traverse through this chapter, let us embrace the power of vulnerability, acknowledging our flaws, and actively working towards becoming better partners, leaders, and servants in God's Kingdom.

Be Quick to Hear

In the realm of relationships, especially those nurtured under the banner of Kingdom building, the art of listening stands as a vital cornerstone. This section, "Be Quick to Hear," unveils the profound significance of not just hearing but actively listening with intention and empathy, particularly in times of challenges. It's an art that goes beyond mere auditory process; it's about understanding, empathizing, and connecting deeply with another's heart and soul.

In a small town, there was a pastor named Samuel, whose wisdom and compassion drew many to his congregation. His ability to listen was legendary; he seemed to not just hear, but to understand and feel the words of those who sought his counsel. One day, a young couple, Thomas and Eliza, members of his church, came to him, their marriage strained under the weight of unmet expectations and frequent misunderstandings. As they spoke, Samuel didn't interrupt, his gaze steady, his demeanor empathetic. He embodied the scripture from James 1:19, "Everyone should be quick to listen, slow to speak and slow to become angry."

Samuel's attentive listening provided a safe space for Thomas and Eliza to express their feelings without fear of judgment or immediate response. This practice of active listening helped him understand the root of their issues, not just the surface emotions. Samuel's approach to listening went beyond mere problem-solving; it was about connecting with the couple on a deeper level, showing them the love and empathy Christ calls us to exhibit.

The transformative power of Samuel's listening soon became evident. Inspired by his example, Thomas and Eliza began to apply active listening in their conversations. They learned to give each other undivided attention, to understand before seeking to be understood. This change in communication led to a significant shift in their relationship. Misunderstandings decreased, empathy increased, and a new level of mutual respect began to grow. They found common ground in their challenges, and solutions became easier to find as they listened to each other with patience and openness.

Moreover, this practice of being quick to hear had a ripple effect in their personal lives and the community. They became better listeners to their friends, family, and colleagues, fostering a culture of empathy and understanding around them. Their experience was a living testament to the power of active listening in building and strengthening relationships.

The art of being quick to hear is a crucial component in navigating the complexities of relationships, especially during challenging times. It's about actively listening to understand, showing empathy, and considering the other person's perspective. This skill fosters effective communication, reduces misunderstandings, and aids in finding common ground, even in the midst of difficulties. As we progress through this chapter, let us embrace the wisdom of being quick to hear, understanding its importance in deepening our relationships and reflecting the love of Christ in our interactions. This approach is not just about solving problems; it's about connecting hearts, building bridges, and nurturing a relationship grounded in mutual respect and understanding.

Be Slow to Anger

The ability to be slow to anger is not just an admirable quality, but a vital element in sustaining and nurturing healthy interactions. This section explores the importance of patience and self-control in times of conflict, emphasizing how these virtues play a crucial role in preventing escalation and fostering constructive resolution.

In a small rural church, there was an elder, Mr. Jacob, renowned for his calm demeanor and wise counsel. His life wasn't devoid of provocations or disagreements; however, his response to these situations was always measured and thoughtful. The story of Mr. Jacob and a new member of the congregation, Paul, who often challenged Mr. Jacob's views during church meetings, offers a vivid illustration of the principle of being slow to anger.

Paul, passionate and often impulsive, would raise points of contention, sometimes in a confrontational tone. Instead of reacting in kind, Mr. Jacob would listen attentively, pausing before responding. His responses were always infused with grace and wisdom, never with anger or frustration. He lived out the essence of James 1:19-20, which says, "Everyone should be quick to listen, slow to speak and slow to become angry, because human anger does not produce the righteousness that God desires."

This approach did more than just diffuse potential arguments. It created an atmosphere of respect and open dialogue within the church community. Mr. Jacob's ability to be slow to anger taught Paul and others the value of thoughtful communication. Paul began to understand that being heard is not about the volume of one's voice but the validity of one's points and the manner in which they are presented.

Moreover, Mr. Jacob's temperament of being slow to anger extended beyond church meetings. It permeated his personal relationships, setting an example for his family and friends. In his marriage, when disagreements arose, his and his wife's commitment to patience and understanding fostered a deeper level of communication and trust. They knew that anger would not guide their discussions; rather, respect and love would lead the way to resolution.

The principle of being slow to anger is not a call to suppress or ignore feelings of frustration or irritation. Rather, it's about managing these emotions in a way that does not hinder constructive dialogue or damage relationships. It's about recognizing that words spoken in anger can leave lasting scars and that patience can pave the way for healing and understanding.

In conclusion, the practice of being slow to anger is a fundamental aspect of navigating the challenges inherent in any relationship. It's about cultivating patience and self-control, especially in the face of provocation. This approach allows for thoughtful and calm responses, which are essential for open dialogue and effective problem-solving. As we reflect on this principle, let us strive to embody this virtue in our interactions, understanding that being slow to anger is not just an individual trait, but a powerful tool that enhances communication, deepens understanding, and strengthens the bonds of our relationships in the service of God's Kingdom.

Be Willing to Step in and Do More Than Your Share

The willingness to step in and do more than one's share is not merely a gracious act; it's a profound expression of love, commitment, and understanding. This section of Chapter 8 delves into the essence of true partnership, where the equilibrium of give-and-take is sometimes tilted by necessity, and one partner may shoulder a heavier burden to support the other.

The story of Martin and Claire, a couple deeply committed to their community and church, paints a vivid picture of this principle. Martin, a diligent and hardworking man, unexpectedly fell ill, leaving him unable to fulfill his usual responsibilities both at home and in their shared ministry work. Claire, recognizing the sudden shift in their circumstances, gracefully stepped up, taking on not only her own tasks but also those of Martin's.

Her actions were a living embodiment of the Biblical principle found in Galatians 6:2, "Carry each other's burdens, and in this way, you will fulfill the law of Christ." Claire's willingness to do more than her share was not about keeping score or expecting something in return; it was a genuine expression of her love for Martin and her dedication to their shared goals and responsibilities.

This period was challenging for Claire, juggling additional responsibilities while also caring for Martin. Yet, she found strength not just in her faith but also in the knowledge that their roles could easily have been reversed, and Martin would have done the same for her. This mutual understanding and unspoken agreement that they were in this together – "for better, for worse" – was the foundation of their relationship.

Moreover, Claire's actions had a ripple effect, inspiring and encouraging others in their community. Her willingness to step in and bear a greater load was a testament to the power of selfless love and service. It served as a reminder to others that in every partnership, there are seasons when one must give more than they receive and that these seasons are opportunities to demonstrate true commitment and compassion.

During Martin's recovery, their relationship grew even stronger. The challenges they faced together, and Claire's willingness to take on more than her share, deepened their mutual respect and love. It highlighted the importance of supporting each other through thick and thin, not as a duty but as a natural extension of their commitment to one another and to their shared purpose in God's Kingdom.

The willingness to step in and do more than your share is a hallmark of true partnership. It is a powerful expression of love, a reflection of commitment, and a reinforcement of the idea that a relationship is not about maintaining a perfect balance but about being there for each other in times of need. This section of the chapter encourages us to look beyond the confines of our responsibilities, to embrace the spirit of service and selflessness, and to remember that in the ups and downs of life, our greatest strength often lies in our ability to support and uplift each other.

Remember There's Always Someone Smarter Than You

In the symphony of life and relationships, the notes of humility play an essential role. This resonates with the wisdom of embracing humility in our interactions, particularly in the face of challenges. It's a humble acknowledgment that we don't possess all the answers and an open invitation to learn from others. This mindset not only enhances personal growth but also enriches relationships with new insights and collaborative solutions.

In a small suburban church, Pastor Helen was known for her deep understanding of scripture and her ability to apply it practically in her sermons. Her insights were often enlightening, and many in her congregation looked up to her. However, Pastor Helen was always the first to admit that her knowledge was not exhaustive. She frequently encouraged her congregation to seek wisdom from various sources and reminded them of Proverbs 12:15, "The way of fools seems right to them, but the wise listen to advice."

This humility and openness to learning were demonstrated vividly when the church faced a financial crisis. Despite her experience, Pastor Helen realized that this was outside her expertise. She sought counsel from a member of the congregation, Mr. James, who had a background in finance. Mr. James provided insights and strategies that Pastor Helen had not considered. Her willingness to acknowledge that someone else had greater knowledge in this area led to innovative solutions that helped steer the church through its financial challenges.

Pastor Helen's approach to this situation fostered a culture of mutual respect and collaboration within the church. It encouraged members of the congregation to value and share their knowledge, understanding that everyone had something to contribute. This atmosphere of learning and collaboration brought about a deeper sense of community and a shared commitment to the church's growth and wellbeing.

Moreover, Pastor Helen's humility in admitting that she did not have all the answers, and her willingness to learn from others, also had a profound impact on her personal relationships. Her family and friends saw her not just as a leader but as someone who valued and respected the knowledge and experience of others. This approach to life and leadership strengthened her connections, fostering deeper bonds based on mutual respect and admiration.

In relationships, whether personal, professional, or spiritual, the understanding that there is always someone smarter can be incredibly freeing. It removes the pressure to be infallible and opens up a world of continuous learning and growth. This mindset encourages partners to value each other's strengths and perspectives, to collaborate on solutions, and to approach challenges with the knowledge that they can learn from each other and from those around them.

Remembering that there is always someone smarter is a powerful principle in navigating the challenges of life and relationships. It's a call to humility, an invitation to continuous learning, and a reminder to value and respect the wisdom of others. As we embrace this principle, we foster a culture of collaboration, enhance our problem-solving abilities, and strengthen the bonds of our relationships. It's a mindset that not only acknowledges our limitations but also celebrates the vastness of collective wisdom and the endless possibilities it brings to our shared journey.

True Partnership is Becoming Acquainted and Maturing Together

At the heart of every meaningful relationship lies the essence of true partnership - a journey of becoming deeply acquainted and maturing together, particularly through the challenges that life invariably presents. This concept transcends the mere division of responsibilities or striving for equality; it's about nurturing a bond that grows and evolves, enriched by experiences and shaped by mutual support, humility, patience, and effective communication.

The story of Michael and Linda, a couple deeply involved in community service, exemplifies this dynamic process of growing and maturing together. When they first met, their connection was immediate, but their journey to becoming true partners involved much more than shared interests and initial compatibility. It was a path marked by learning, adjusting, and growing, not just as individuals but as a cohesive unit.

Early in their marriage, they faced a significant challenge when they undertook the responsibility of caring for a relative with a chronic illness. This situation tested their patience, communication, and understanding of each other's strengths and weaknesses. During this time, they turned to scriptures like Ecclesiastes 4:9-10, "Two are better than one because they have a good return for their labor: If either of them falls down, one can help the other up. But pity anyone who falls and has no one to help them up." These verses became a source of strength and reminder of the importance of supporting each other.

This experience became a pivotal point in their relationship. It taught them the importance of working together, leaning on each other's strengths, and compensating for each other's weaknesses. It wasn't about keeping score or maintaining an exact balance, but about filling in for each other when needed, offering support, and growing in understanding and empathy.

Their journey also involved developing a deep acquaintance with each other's emotional landscapes, dreams, fears, and aspirations. Through open and honest communication, they learned to express their feelings effectively, listen actively, and resolve conflicts in a way that strengthened rather than weakened their bond. They discovered that true partnership is as much about understanding each other's silences as it is about engaging in conversations.

Moreover, Michael and Linda's commitment to growing and maturing together extended to their spiritual lives. They made it a priority to pray together, study the Bible, and actively participate in their church community. These spiritual practices not only deepened their faith but also reinforced their bond. They learned to view their relationship not just in the context of their personal happiness but as a testimony of God's love and grace.

Their story teaches that true partnership in relationships is a continuous process of becoming more deeply acquainted with each other and maturing together, especially through challenges. This process requires humility to admit mistakes, patience to understand differences, effective communication to express thoughts and feelings, and a willingness to support each other unconditionally.

True partnership, as Michael and Linda's story illustrates, is about embracing the principles of mutual growth, understanding, and support. It's about building a relationship that is resilient, fulfilling, and reflective of the unity and love central to the Kingdom of God. As couples and partners embark on this journey, they forge a bond that is not only enduring but also enriching, both for themselves and for the community around them. This journey, though filled with its share of challenges, is a beautiful testament to the power of love, commitment, and shared growth.

As we reach the end of Chapter 8, it becomes increasingly clear that the essence of true partnership in relationships is intricately shaped through the shared experiences of facing challenges and embracing growth together. This journey, though often marked by trials and tribulations, serves as the crucible in which resilience is forged and connections in Christ are deepened. Throughout this chapter, we have navigated various aspects of partnership, from the humility of admitting our shortcomings to the strength found in being quick to hear and slow to anger, and the profound impact of stepping in to bear more than our share when needed.

This exploration has highlighted that partnerships are not static entities but dynamic and evolving bonds, strengthened not just in moments of harmony but significantly so in times of adversity. As we traverse through conflicts and challenges, the true depth of our relationships is revealed and tested. It's in these moments that the foundations of patience, understanding, mutual support, and effective communication are proven crucial.

Moreover, this chapter has reaffirmed that the growth and resilience developed in our relationships have a broader impact than on the partnerships alone. They extend into our communities, our ministries, and our personal walks with Christ. As we grow together with our partners, we become more effective in our collective service to the Kingdom of God, embodying the unity and love that Christ himself prayed for in John 17:21, "That they all may be one, as You, Father, are in Me, and I in You; that they also may be one in Us, that the world may believe that You sent Me."

In conclusion, the journey of true partnership in relationships is a testament to the transformative power of facing challenges and growing together. It's a journey that not only strengthens our bonds with each other but also deepens our connection with Christ. As we close this chapter, let us carry forward the lessons learned and the wisdom gained, embracing every opportunity to forge stronger, more resilient relationships, rooted in love, nurtured through challenges, and flourishing in the grace and knowledge of Jesus Christ.

Chapter 9

Leadership in Kingdom Building

Welcome to Chapter 9, where we delve into the profound realm of leadership within the context of Kingdom building. This chapter is dedicated to exploring the essential qualities that define a Kingdom leader, emphasizing the pivotal roles of humility, service, inclusivity, and empowerment. In the Kingdom context, leadership is not merely about directing or commanding; it is about guiding and nurturing others towards a common purpose.

This chapter aims to illuminate how a Kingdom leader differentiates from conventional leadership paradigms. We will explore the significance of humility in leadership - understanding that true leadership stems not from a desire for personal glory but from a selfless commitment to serve others. The chapter will highlight how a servant leader prioritizes the needs of their community and leads by example, setting a standard for others to follow.

Inclusivity is another cornerstone of Kingdom leadership. Here, we will discuss the importance of embracing diversity and fostering a sense of belonging among all members of the community. This approach ensures that everyone's voice is heard and valued, thereby strengthening the collective purpose.

Furthermore, we will delve into the concept of empowerment, examining how effective leaders equip and inspire their followers to reach their full potential. By empowering others, Kingdom leaders multiply their impact and further the reach of their collective mission.

This chapter is an invitation to step into the shoes of a Kingdom leader, to understand their mindset, and to embrace their approach to building a stronger, more unified community aligned with God's purpose. Join us on this journey to uncover the essence of leadership in Kingdom building.

Good Leaders are Never Afraid to Raise Up Other Leaders

In the journey of Kingdom Building, the role of a leader transcends conventional boundaries. A true leader in God's Kingdom, imbued with humility and service, understands the profound impact of nurturing and developing new leaders. This path of leadership isn't just about leading; it's about multiplying leadership.

Consider Moses, a humble shepherd turned leader, who led the Israelites out of Egypt. His story, especially in Exodus 18, is a shining example. Jethro, his father-in-law, advised him to delegate responsibilities to capable men. This act wasn't a sign of weakness but of strength and wisdom. Moses raised leaders, equipping them to handle smaller matters, thus ensuring that the community thrived under a shared leadership model.

Similarly, Jesus Christ himself exemplified this principle in the most remarkable way. He didn't keep his wisdom and power to himself; instead, he called the twelve disciples. He invested in them, taught them, and empowered them. As seen in Matthew 28:19-20, He entrusted them with the Great Commission, to go and make disciples of all nations. Jesus didn't just build a following; he built leaders who would continue his work long after he ascended to heaven.

In the realm of Kingdom Building, good leaders recognize that their true legacy is not in the number of followers they amass but in the leaders they raise. They create an environment where others are encouraged to grow, take on responsibilities, and flourish in their own leadership journeys. This nurturing process is akin to a gardener who plants, waters, and tends to young saplings, knowing that these trees will one day bear their own fruit and provide shade to others.

The Apostle Paul, in his relationship with Timothy, illustrates this beautifully. He didn't just mentor Timothy; he empowered him, giving him significant responsibilities in the early church. In his letters, Paul often encourages Timothy to be strong, to teach, and to endure hardship (2 Timothy 2:1-2). He saw the potential in Timothy and nurtured it, setting an example for leadership in the Kingdom.

This leadership style creates a ripple effect of growth and empowerment. When leaders focus on raising other leaders, they set in motion a cycle of continual growth and expansion of God's Kingdom. It's about creating a legacy that outlives one's tenure, a legacy of empowered individuals who carry the torch forward with the same spirit of humility and service.

Therefore, in God's Kingdom, the greatest leaders are those who see beyond their tenure, who envision and work towards a future where their influence is multiplied through the leaders they raise. This chapter celebrates and explores this selfless and visionary aspect of leadership, a cornerstone in the grand design of Kingdom Building.

Don't Take on Everything If Others Are Willing to Help You

In the heart of effective Kingdom leadership lies a simple yet profound truth: don't shoulder every burden alone when others are ready and willing to share the load. This principle isn't just about lightening the leader's load; it's a strategic approach that empowers others, cultivates growth, and builds a robust, capable team.

Picture a community where each member's unique talents and abilities are recognized and utilized. Here, a leader doesn't stand alone at the helm, juggling every task. Instead, they act as a conductor, orchestrating a symphony of diverse skills and strengths. This environment not only prevents the leader's burnout but also instills a sense of ownership and pride among team members as they contribute to their community's success.

Delegation is seen in the story of the early church in the Book of Acts. The Apostles, overwhelmed by the growing needs of their community, chose seven men to oversee the distribution of food (Acts 6:1-6). This decision allowed the Apostles to focus on prayer and ministry of the word. It's a classic example of leaders recognizing they couldn't — and shouldn't — do it all. They identified capable individuals, entrusted them with responsibilities, and in doing so, strengthened the whole community.

This approach resonates with the wisdom of Proverbs 15:22, which says, "Plans fail for lack of counsel, but with many advisers they succeed." Leaders who embrace this wisdom understand the power of collective effort. They know that sharing responsibilities isn't a sign of weakness, but a strategic move that leverages diverse capabilities for the greater good.

Furthermore, when leaders delegate, they create opportunities for growth. It's an expression of trust that can be incredibly motivating. People tend to rise to the occasion when given a chance, bringing forth creativity and solutions that might otherwise remain untapped. As these individuals grow, the entire community benefits from their expanded capabilities and fresh perspectives.

In essence, refusing to take on everything and instead, sharing responsibilities, is a hallmark of visionary leadership. It reflects an understanding that true strength lies in unity and shared purpose. By delegating, leaders not only prevent their own burnout but also foster an environment where everyone feels valued and invested in the collective mission. It's about building a team where each member is encouraged to shine, contributing their best to the overarching goal of Kingdom Building.

Identify Gifts in Others & Distribute the Workload Equally

One of the most critical skills in effective leadership, especially in the realm of Kingdom Building, is the keen ability to discern and nurture the diverse gifts and talents present within a community. It's about seeing beyond the surface, identifying the unique capabilities each individual brings, and aligning tasks with their innate strengths. This approach ensures that the workload is not just evenly distributed, but also strategically allocated, enhancing the overall efficiency and cohesiveness of the team.

Consider the scenario of a community project. A wise leader takes the time to understand their team members: one might have a gift for organization, another for communication, while a third might excel in creative problem-solving. By assigning responsibilities that align with these gifts, the leader ensures that each task is handled by someone who is not just capable, but also passionate about that particular aspect of work. This methodology transforms a routine project into a vibrant tapestry of collaborative effort, where each contribution is significant and perfectly placed.

This principle mirrors the Apostle Paul's teachings in 1 Corinthians 12:4-6, where he speaks of different gifts but the same Spirit, different services but the same Lord, and different workings but the same God. Paul emphasizes the diversity of gifts within a community and the importance of each in contributing to the common good. By recognizing and utilizing these varied gifts, leaders in the Kingdom ensure that each member of their community is not only contributing but flourishing in their role.

Furthermore, this equitable distribution of work goes a long way in fostering a sense of belonging and value among team members. When individuals see that their unique talents are recognized and utilized, it boosts their confidence and commitment to the group's objectives. They feel genuinely valued, not just as workers but as integral parts of the community, each playing a critical role in the collective mission.

In essence, the ability to identify and utilize the gifts of others is a testament to a leader's insight and compassion. It's about seeing the potential in each individual and creating an environment where this potential can be realized and celebrated. Such leadership not only drives efficiency and success in projects but also nurtures a community where everyone feels seen, valued, and essential to the Kingdom's work.

Keep the Vision Before You

Holding fast to a clear vision is the linchpin of effective leadership. This unwavering focus on the mission is not just a guide; it is a source of inspiration, a constant reminder of the greater purpose that unites and drives the entire team.

Let's turn the pages of the Bible to Nehemiah, a leader whose story epitomizes the power of a steadfast vision. When Nehemiah heard about the broken walls of Jerusalem, he was moved to act. This vision of rebuilding the walls wasn't just a construction project; it was a symbol of restoration and hope for the people. Throughout the arduous task, Nehemiah faced opposition and discouragement, but his clarity of vision never wavered. His unwavering commitment inspired the people, and together, they completed the monumental task in a remarkably short time. Nehemiah's story, particularly in Nehemiah 2:17-20, showcases how a clear vision can rally people and spur them to remarkable achievements.

Similarly, Jesus Christ, the ultimate example of visionary leadership, consistently communicated His mission to His disciples. His teachings and parables were more than moral lessons; they were insights into the Kingdom of Heaven. He painted a picture of the Kingdom so vividly that His followers were willing to leave everything behind and follow Him. This vision was so compelling that it continued to guide the early church long after His ascension, as seen in Acts and the Epistles.

For leaders in the realm of Kingdom Building, keeping the vision at the forefront is crucial. It means regularly reminding the team of the 'why' behind their efforts. It's about creating a culture where the shared goals are not just understood but are a part of the team's DNA. Leaders achieve this through their words and actions, consistently aligning their guidance and decisions with the vision. They understand that a team aligned with a powerful vision can overcome significant challenges and achieve extraordinary results.

This principle goes beyond mere repetition of goals. It's about making the vision so palpable that each team member can see their role in it. Like a masterful composer who ensures each musician understands not only their part but how it contributes to the symphony, effective leaders help their team members see how their individual efforts contribute to the overarching purpose.

In essence, "Keep the Vision Before You" is more than a mantra; it's a strategic approach to leadership. It ensures that every step taken is a step toward the realization of the Kingdom's goals. It is about leading with conviction and passion, ensuring that the vision remains alive and vibrant, guiding and inspiring the team towards collective success in their sacred mission.

Don't Mimic What Others Are Doing; Be Strategic

In the landscape of Kingdom Building, the role of a leader often calls for innovation and a tailored strategy, rather than a one-size-fits-all approach. This distinction is vital: what succeeds in one context might not in another. Effective leaders recognize this and craft strategies that resonate with their unique situation, ensuring their efforts are both meaningful and impactful.

The biblical account of David facing Goliath in 1 Samuel 17 offers a striking illustration of this principle. When David prepared to confront the giant, King Saul offered him his armor. However, David chose not to wear it, realizing it was cumbersome and unfamiliar to him. Instead, he went with his sling and stones, tools he was skilled with. David's strategic choice, grounded in his own strengths and experiences, led to an unlikely but historic victory. This story underlines the importance of not blindly adopting others' methods but instead finding what works best for the unique challenges and strengths at hand.

Similarly, when Jesus sent out his disciples in Matthew 10, He didn't give them a generic blueprint to follow in their ministry. Instead, He provided specific instructions tailored to their mission and context. He advised them on how to approach different towns, how to interact with people, and even how to respond to rejection. Jesus understood that each mission field was different, and He equipped

His disciples with strategies that would be most effective in their specific circumstances.

Good leadership in Kingdom Building, therefore, is about being discerning and intentional in strategy development. It involves a deep understanding of the context — the community's needs, the available resources, and the unique dynamics at play. A strategic leader takes time to assess these factors and crafts an approach that is not only innovative but also aligned with the mission's goals.

This approach ensures that efforts are not wasted on methods that may not suit the context. Instead, resources are utilized in the most effective way possible, and the impact of the work is maximized. A strategic leader also inspires creativity and resourcefulness within the team, encouraging members to think outside the box and contribute their ideas.

In summary, "Don't Mimic What Others Are Doing; Be Strategic" is a call to leadership that is thoughtful, context-aware, and innovative. It's about understanding that the path to achieving Kingdom goals is not always a well-trodden one; sometimes, it requires forging a new way, tailored to the specific journey God has set before you and your team. This bespoke approach not only ensures effectiveness and impact but also fosters a sense of authenticity and purpose in the work of Kingdom Building.

Live & Encourage a Balanced Lifestyle

leaders are not just architects of the mission; they are also the caretakers of their team's well-being. A crucial aspect of this leadership involves modeling and fostering a balanced lifestyle, one that harmoniously blends work, spiritual growth, emotional wellness, and physical health.

The life of Jesus Christ offers profound insights into this balance. Amidst his profound ministry, Jesus often took time to retreat and pray, as seen in Mark 1:35, where He rose early to find a solitary place to commune with the Father. He knew the value of solitude and reflection in maintaining His spiritual and emotional health, setting an example for all leaders. Jesus also understood the importance of community and fellowship, often dining and conversing with His disciples and others, nurturing not just spiritual truths but relationships as well.

Likewise, in the Old Testament, the principle of the Sabbath, as outlined in Exodus 20:8-10, underscores the importance God places on rest. It is a divine directive to pause from work, to rejuvenate, and to reflect. This concept is more than just a day of rest; it is a paradigm for maintaining balance in life, ensuring that one's work, spiritual practices, and personal life are in harmony.

Leaders in Kingdom Building, by living out this balance, become beacons of sustainable commitment. When they prioritize not only their own well-being but also encourage their team to do the same, they foster an environment where burnout is mitigated, and long-term dedication is viable. It's about understanding that the well-being of each member is integral to the health and success of the entire mission.

Moreover, a balanced lifestyle cultivates a sense of joy and fulfillment. When team members see their leader valuing their life outside of work, it gives them permission to do the same, creating a more vibrant and supportive community. This approach also acknowledges and respects the multi-faceted nature of each individual - as beings who are spiritual, emotional, physical, and intellectual.

Encouraging a balanced lifestyle involves intentional actions - like setting boundaries for work hours, creating opportunities for spiritual and emotional growth, and encouraging physical health. It's about creating a culture where taking time for self-care is not seen as a luxury, but a necessity for holistic living.

In essence, "Live & Encourage a Balanced Lifestyle" is a call to Kingdom leaders to be mindful stewards of their own lives and those they lead. It's an invitation to weave a pattern of life that balances the zeal for the mission with the need for personal rejuvenation and growth. By embodying this balance, leaders not only enhance their own effectiveness but also inspire their team to embrace a lifestyle that supports long-term happiness, health, and productivity in the grand endeavor of Kingdom Building.

Good Leaders Do Not Compete; They Collaborate

The essence of true leadership is found not in competition but in collaboration. This principle, rooted in the wisdom of the Scriptures, transforms the conventional view of leadership into one that cherishes unity and collective effort for the fulfillment of God's purpose.

Reflect on the early church as described in Acts 2:42-47. Here, believers lived in a community marked by unity and sharing. They broke bread in their homes, ate together with glad and sincere hearts, praising God. This wasn't just a group of individuals; it was a united body where each member worked collaboratively for the common good. This environment of mutual support and collaboration was key to their strength and growth.

Similarly, in 1 Corinthians 3:6-7, Paul talks about planting the seed and Apollos watering it, but God making it grow. This analogy beautifully captures the essence of collaborative leadership. It's not about who does the most or who gets the credit; it's about working together in different roles towards a common goal. In God's Kingdom, every effort, no matter how small, contributes to the overall purpose.

Effective leaders in Kingdom Building embrace this model. They understand that success is not about outshining others but about shining together. Such leaders focus on building and empowering their team, sharing knowledge and resources generously. They create a culture where collaboration is valued over competition, where each member is encouraged to contribute their best in unison with others.

This approach is grounded in humility, service, and inclusivity. Leaders who collaborate well are those who humbly recognize their need for others, who serve their team by fostering an environment of open communication and mutual respect, and who include all members in the journey, valuing diverse perspectives and skills.

By fostering collaboration, these leaders inspire and mobilize others towards fulfilling God's purpose. They create a harmonious, effective environment where the collective efforts supersede individual accomplishments. It's a setting where each victory is shared, each challenge is faced together, and the overall mission thrives not on individual prowess but on the combined strengths of the team.

This is a profound call to action for those in Kingdom Building leadership. It's an invitation to lead in a way that exemplifies the unity and collaboration inherent in God's plan for His people. By embracing this principle, leaders ensure that the work is done not just effectively, but also in a way that reflects the harmony and unity that is at the heart of the Kingdom of God.

As we conclude this exploration of Chapter 9, we find ourselves deeply inspired by the profoundly collaborative and growth-oriented essence of Kingdom leadership. This journey we've embarked on is far from a path marked by competition and solitary achievements. Instead, it is a road of mutual elevation, a collective ascent where we inspire and uplift each other towards a shared divine purpose.

Kingdom leadership, as we've seen, is about much more than just guiding others; it's about fostering an environment where every individual can thrive. It's a leadership style that embraces the gifts and talents of each person, aligning them in a way that not only furthers the mission but also enhances personal growth and fulfillment. This approach transforms the very concept of leadership from being a role of authority to one of service and empowerment.

In this chapter, we've delved into the nuances of such leadership, understanding that true Kingdom leaders are those who walk alongside their team, not ahead of them. They are visionaries who keep the overarching goals in sight, yet are adaptable, tailoring their strategies to fit the unique needs and strengths of their community. These leaders understand that their legacy lies not in the monuments they build, but in the people they nurture and the leaders they develop.

We've also learned that effective Kingdom leadership involves living and promoting a balanced lifestyle, recognizing that the health and well-being of each team member are integral to the success of the collective mission. It's about cultivating an environment where work, spiritual growth, and personal well-being are in harmony, creating a sustainable model for long-term success and happiness.

As we move forward from this chapter, let us carry these insights with us, applying them to our own journeys in leadership. May we strive to be leaders who not only strive for the success of our endeavors but also for the flourishing of the people we are privileged to lead. In doing so, we honor the true spirit of Kingdom Building, creating a legacy that resonates with love, service, and collaborative success.

Chapter 10

Community Outreach and Impact

In the heart of every thriving society lies the spirit of community — a bond that not only unites us but also calls us to action in the service of others. "Thy Kingdom Come" has journeyed through the pathways of personal development and relationship building, emphasizing our divine call to connect deeply with those around us. Now, in Chapter 10, we turn our focus outward, to the broader community, delving into the critical aspect of understanding and addressing community needs through outreach. This chapter serves as a guide to impactful community service, reflecting the inclusive and loving heart of God's Kingdom.

Community outreach is not just an activity; it's a manifestation of our faith and love in action. It is how we embody the teachings of Christ, who reached out to the marginalized, healed the sick, and embraced the outcast. Our call to serve is a call to mirror this example, to step into the world with a heart of compassion and hands ready to help. In doing so, we not only meet the physical and emotional needs of those around us but also bear witness to the transformative power of God's love in our lives and in our communities.

Understanding community needs requires a willingness to listen and learn. It's about stepping into the lives of others, hearing their stories, and recognizing the challenges they face. This chapter will explore various methods of identifying these needs, from community surveys to personal engagement. We will discuss the importance of empathy and cultural sensitivity in this process, ensuring that our efforts are both respectful and relevant.

The impact of community service is multifaceted. Not only does it provide tangible help and support to those in need, but it also fosters a sense of belonging and solidarity within the community. This chapter will showcase inspiring examples of community outreach initiatives that have made a significant difference in their communities. From food banks and clothing drives to mentorship programs and environmental projects, we will examine the varied ways in which individuals and groups can contribute to the welfare of their community.

Furthermore, we'll delve into the concept of servant leadership in community outreach. True leadership is not about authority or power; it's about serving others selflessly and leading by example. We will explore how to cultivate these leadership qualities within ourselves and inspire others to join in community service.

Collaboration is key in effective community outreach. This chapter will guide you in building partnerships with local organizations, churches, and other groups that share a common vision for community improvement. By working together, we can amplify our impact and bring about more substantial and sustainable change.

As we journey through this chapter, let's remember that community outreach is an ongoing process. It's about building relationships, understanding needs, and responding with love and action. As members of God's Kingdom, we are called to be agents of change, bringing hope and light into our communities. Let us embrace this call with enthusiasm and dedication, knowing that through our efforts, God's Kingdom is reflected on earth.

In Order to Have a Successful Community Outreach, You Must Find the Needs of Your Community

True partnership in community outreach is not just about meeting needs; it's a journey of becoming acquainted and maturing together. This process echoes the teachings of the Bible, where Paul speaks of the body of Christ, each member with its own role, yet all essential (1 Corinthians 12:12-27). Likewise, our communities are bodies composed of diverse yet interconnected individuals. Understanding these individuals and their needs is not merely a task—it's a calling to enter into each other's stories, to grow and learn together.

Let us reflect on the story of Nehemiah, a leader who effectively identified the needs of his community. When Nehemiah heard about the plight of the Jerusalem walls, he didn't launch into action immediately. He wept, prayed, and fasted (Nehemiah 1:4). He took time to understand the depth of the problem. This contemplation led him to approach King Artaxerxes, not with a brash plan, but with a heart full of compassion and a clear understanding of what his community needed.

This Biblical example teaches us a vital lesson: successful community outreach requires an intimate understanding of the community's heart. It's about walking the streets, listening to the stories of its people, understanding their struggles and joys. As we do this, we begin to see beyond the surface needs. We discover a deeper layer of emotional, spiritual, and physical requirements that are often intertwined.

In one community, the need might be for a youth mentoring program; in another, it might be a food bank or support for the elderly. Each community is unique, and its needs are equally so. It's about going deeper, asking questions, and understanding the 'whys' behind the 'whats'. Proverbs 3:27 reminds us, "Do not withhold good from those to whom it is due, when it is in your power to act." This proverb is a call to action, rooted in understanding and empathy.

As we identify these needs, we must remember that outreach is not just about giving; it's about building relationships. It's about becoming a part of the community's fabric, weaving together stories of hope, resilience, and faith. In doing so, we reflect the words of Jesus in Matthew 25:40, "Truly I tell you, whatever you did for one of the least of these brothers and sisters of mine, you did for me."

Consider the church that started a community garden. Initially, it was just to provide fresh produce to those in need. But as church members worked side by side with community members, stories were shared, relationships were forged, and the garden became a place of communal healing and connection. It wasn't just vegetables that grew in that garden, but trust, understanding, and companionship.

In this journey, we are not just dispensers of aid, but partners in growth. We learn from the community as much as they might learn from us. We grow in understanding, compassion, and love. This is the heart of successful community outreach – a partnership that blossoms over time, rooted in mutual respect and a genuine desire to see each other thrive.

As we embark on this journey of outreach, let us do so with open hearts and minds, ready to be taught and transformed by those we seek to serve. For in this process, we are not only meeting the needs of a community; we are becoming a part of it, maturing together in the light of God's love and purpose.

Speak to Your Neighbors

The art of conversation, often overlooked, is a powerful tool in understanding and serving our communities. In this section, we explore the significance of engaging in dialogues with our neighbors, an approach deeply rooted in the Biblical principle of love and fellowship.

Consider the story of Jesus and the Samaritan woman at the well (John 4:1-42). Jesus, by simply initiating a conversation, broke cultural barriers and transformed a life. Through this exchange, Jesus not only addressed the woman's immediate needs but also touched her life profoundly, leading to a ripple effect in her community. This encounter exemplifies the transformative power of speaking to our neighbors with intention and compassion.

In a quiet neighborhood, there lived an elderly woman named Mrs. Johnson. She rarely left her house, and the neighbors knew little about her. One day, a group from a local church, seeking to understand how they could serve their community better, decided to visit her. With no agenda other than to listen, they knocked on her door. Mrs. Johnson, surprised and a little wary, let them in.

As they spoke, Mrs. Johnson shared stories of her youth, her family, and her current struggles with loneliness and mobility. This conversation revealed a need that was not visible from the outside: the need for companionship and assistance with everyday tasks. Inspired by this encounter, the church members began a program where volunteers would visit elderly members of the community, offering companionship and help with household chores. This program didn't just meet practical needs; it fostered a sense of belonging and community.

Proverbs 18:13 teaches, "To answer before listening—that is folly and shame." This wisdom underscores the importance of listening as a fundamental part of understanding. By speaking to our neighbors, we open doors to their lives and hearts. We learn about the single mother struggling to balance work and childcare, the teenager grappling with identity and belonging, or the immigrant family facing language barriers.

As Kingdom builders, our outreach must be grounded in genuine relationships. When we listen to our neighbors, we honor their experiences and affirm their value. James 1:19 advises us, "Everyone should be quick to listen, slow to speak and slow to become angry." This guidance is crucial in our approach to community outreach. In listening, we often find that the needs of our communities are more profound than we initially perceive.

The process of speaking to neighbors also invites us into a journey of self-discovery and spiritual growth. As we engage with diverse stories and experiences, our own perspectives broaden, and our understanding deepens. Through these conversations, we are often reminded of the call in Galatians 6:2, "Carry each other's burdens, and in this way, you will fulfill the law of Christ."

Speaking to our neighbors is not a mere outreach strategy; it is a call to embody the love and empathy of Christ. It is an invitation to enter into the lives of those around us, to share in their joys and struggles, and to respond with compassion and action. As we undertake this journey, let us do so with open hearts, ready to listen, learn, and serve in the way that truly reflects the Kingdom of God.

Communicate with Successful Community Outreaches to Form Relationships and Collaborations

the wisdom and experiences of those who have tread the path before us are invaluable. The Bible reminds us in Proverbs 15:22, "Plans fail for lack of counsel, but with many advisers they succeed." This principle is crucial when we embark on community outreach initiatives. Communicating with organizations that have established successful programs provides a treasure trove of insights and opportunities for collaboration.

Consider the story of a small church in a bustling city. They had a vision to start a program to feed the homeless but had little experience in such endeavors. Rather than attempting this on their own, they reached out to a nearby church known for its successful soup kitchen. The leaders of the two churches met, sharing stories, challenges, and wisdom. The experienced church leaders spoke of their early struggles, the lessons they learned about organizing volunteers, sourcing food, and connecting with those they served.

This collaboration brought to life Ecclesiastes 4:9, "Two are better than one, because they have a good return for their labor." The established church provided guidance on how to set up the program, avoid waste, and create a welcoming environment. They even offered to train the new volunteers. This partnership not only expedited the process but also fostered a bond between the two congregations.

There's also the story of a youth mentorship program in a small town. When the program initially struggled to engage the local youth, the coordinators reached out to a successful mentorship program in a neighboring town. Through this communication, they discovered new engagement strategies, including involving local businesses and schools, and adapting activities to better suit the interests of their youth. This sharing of knowledge and resources exemplified the spirit of collaboration highlighted in Philippians 2:4, "Not looking to your own interests but each of you to the interests of the others."

In another instance, a group aimed to start a literacy program but had limited resources. By reaching out to a well-established literacy program in another city, they learned cost-effective methods and received donations of books and materials. This gesture of generosity was a reflection of the teaching in Hebrews 13:16, "And do not forget to do good and to share with others, for with such sacrifices God is pleased."

These stories highlight the importance of communication and collaboration in community outreach. When we seek the counsel and partnership of those with experience, we open ourselves to a wealth of knowledge and resources. This approach not only enhances the effectiveness of new initiatives but also fosters unity and strength in the broader community of faith.

In forming these relationships and collaborations, we must approach with humility, ready to learn and adapt. It's also essential to maintain a spirit of gratitude and mutual respect, acknowledging the contributions of each partner. As we engage with successful community outreaches, we weave together a network of support and wisdom, amplifying our impact and extending the reach of God's love through our collective efforts.

Communicating with successful community outreaches to form relationships and collaborations is not just a strategy; it's a biblical principle of wisdom, unity, and shared purpose. It is through these connections that we can build more effective, impactful, and sustainable outreach programs, embodying the collaborative spirit of the Kingdom of God.

Look into Your Local Salvation Army

The story of the Salvation Army is a testament to the power of faith in action, resonating deeply with the teachings of Jesus Christ, who called us to serve the least among us. In Matthew 25:35-36, Jesus says, "For I was hungry and you gave me something to eat, I was thirsty and you gave me something to drink, I was a stranger and you invited me in, I needed clothes and you clothed me, I was sick and you looked after me, I was in prison and you came to visit me." The Salvation Army embodies this call, reaching out to those in need with a variety of programs that provide not just physical aid, but emotional and spiritual support as well.

In a small town, there was a family struggling to make ends meet. The father had lost his job, and the mother was battling illness. As winter approached, the family's challenges seemed insurmountable. It was then that they learned about the local Salvation Army's program for providing winter coats and food assistance. When they visited the Salvation Army, they were greeted with warmth and compassion. Not only did they receive the coats and food they desperately needed, but they also found a community of support. Volunteers listened to their story, offered words of encouragement, and prayed with them, embodying the love of Christ.

This family's experience is one of countless stories of how the Salvation Army meets diverse needs. From providing shelter for the homeless, assisting disaster victims, to offering addiction recovery programs, the Salvation Army serves as a beacon of hope. By observing and engaging with the local Salvation Army, community members and church groups can learn valuable lessons in how to effectively meet the needs of those around them.

The Salvation Army's approach is holistic. They don't just address the immediate need; they also seek to understand the underlying issues and provide long-term support. This method reflects the Biblical principle found in 1 Thessalonians 5:11, "Therefore encourage one another and build each other up, just as in fact you are doing." It's about more than just alleviating physical poverty; it's about nurturing spiritual and emotional well-being.

Exploring the work of the Salvation Army can inspire and guide individuals and churches in their own community outreach efforts. By volunteering with the Salvation Army or even just visiting their facilities, one can witness firsthand the impact of comprehensive care and love in action. The lessons learned here—of compassion, perseverance, and holistic support—can then be applied to other outreach initiatives, amplifying their effectiveness and reach.

Looking into your local Salvation Army is not just about observing an organization in action; it's about learning from a legacy of faith-driven service. It's an opportunity to understand how to meet diverse needs effectively, and how to offer not just aid, but hope and love, following the example of Christ in serving and uplifting our communities.

Boys and Girls Club

The Boys and Girls Club stands as a shining example of commitment to nurturing the younger generation, aligning seamlessly with the Biblical ethos of guiding and supporting children. In the words of Proverbs 22:6, "Start children off on the way they should go, and even when they are old they will not turn from it." This verse captures the essence of the mission of the Boys and Girls Club: to provide a foundation for youth that guides them throughout their lives.

Imagine a bustling community center where the laughter and chatter of children fill the air. Here, in a small town, the local Boys and Girls Club has become a second home for many children and teenagers. Each day, as the school bell rings, a stream of young people make their way to the club. They are greeted by warm smiles and an environment that fosters growth, learning, and safety.

The story of Maria, a volunteer at the club, is particularly moving. Maria, once a shy teenager who found refuge and support at the Boys and Girls Club, now returns as a mentor. She remembers the sense of belonging and encouragement she received, which helped her overcome challenges and pursue her dreams. Now, she's determined to give back, guiding the young members with the same love and support she once received.

The Club's focus on providing a supportive space for children is crucial. In a world fraught with challenges and distractions, these safe havens are essential for nurturing the physical, emotional, and intellectual development of young people. The activities and programs offered — from academic help to sports and arts — cater to diverse interests and needs, ensuring that each child finds a place where they belong.

The impact of the Boys and Girls Club extends beyond the walls of the club itself. It is about instilling values and skills that children carry into their communities and future lives. This aligns with the teachings in Matthew 19:14, where Jesus said, "Let the little children come to me, and do not hinder them, for the kingdom of heaven belongs to such as these." The Club's work is a reflection of this invitation, welcoming all children and offering them a foundation of love, learning, and growth.

For churches and individuals seeking to impact their communities, the Boys and Girls Club offers an inspiring model. It shows the profound difference that can be made by investing time, resources, and heart into the lives of young people. By supporting or partnering with such organizations, or even creating similar programs, we can actively participate in shaping a brighter, more hopeful future for the next generation.

The Boys and Girls Club is more than just an organization; it's a beacon of hope and a model of love in action. Its commitment to supporting and nurturing the youth is a vivid example of the impact we can have when we invest in the younger generation, echoing the Biblical call to guide and uplift the children in our midst.

YMCA

The YMCA, a beacon of holistic development, echoes the Biblical principle of nurturing the whole person. In 1 Thessalonians 5:23, Paul prays that God may "sanctify you through and through. May your whole spirit, soul and body be kept blameless at the coming of our Lord Jesus Christ." This verse encapsulates the YMCA's mission: to foster growth in every aspect of an individual's being – physical, mental, and spiritual.

In a mid-sized city, the YMCA stands as a cornerstone of the community. Its doors open wide to welcome people from all walks of life, offering more than just fitness facilities. It's a place where young and old alike can find enrichment, connection, and support.

Take the story of James, a teenager who found a second home at the YMCA. Struggling with academic pressure and social anxiety, James first stepped into the YMCA for a basketball game. However, what he found was much more than a sports facility. He found mentors who offered guidance, programs that supported his learning, and peers who shared similar struggles and aspirations. The YMCA provided James with a balanced environment where his physical health was nurtured through sports, his mental well-being was supported through educational programs, and his spiritual growth was fostered through community engagement and values-based activities.

Similarly, consider Sarah, a senior citizen who frequents the YMCA's wellness programs. For Sarah, the YMCA is more than just a place to exercise; it's a community where she finds companionship and engages in activities that enrich her spirit. Here, she participates in group exercises, attends wellness workshops, and volunteers in community events, staying active not just physically but also socially and spiritually.

The YMCA's approach to community outreach is a testament to its commitment to comprehensive well-being. Their programs, ranging from youth development initiatives to health and wellness activities for all ages, are designed to cater to the diverse needs of the community. By understanding and implementing the YMCA's model, churches and community leaders can develop outreach programs that do not focus solely on one aspect of well-being but embrace the complexity of human needs.

Furthermore, the YMCA's success lies in its ability to create an inclusive environment where everyone feels welcome and valued. This aligns with the teaching of Galatians 3:28, "There is neither Jew nor Gentile, neither slave nor free, nor is there male and female, for you are all one in Christ Jesus." In a similar vein, the YMCA fosters a sense of unity and belonging, transcending social, economic, and cultural barriers.

The YMCA serves as a vibrant model for community outreach, demonstrating the power and impact of addressing the holistic needs of individuals. By learning from their approach, those involved in Kingdom building can develop comprehensive programs that not only meet physical needs but also enrich mental and spiritual well-being, embodying the Biblical call to care for the whole person.

In The Kingdom, There Are No Big "I's" and Little "You's". We Are All in This Together.

In the realm of community outreach, the concept of unity and equality is paramount. This idea is deeply rooted in the teachings of the Bible, as exemplified in Galatians 3:28, "There is neither Jew nor Greek, slave nor free, male nor female, for you are all one in Christ Jesus." In God's Kingdom, distinctions that often divide people in society lose their significance; what matters is the collective spirit of love, service, and unity.

Let us take a journey to a small community where a church decided to initiate a neighborhood clean-up project. The project was simple

– to bring people together to beautify their community. Initially, the task seemed daunting, with litter-strewn parks and graffiti-covered walls. However, as word spread, something remarkable happened. People from all walks of life began to come forward - the young and old, the affluent and the less fortunate, each bringing their unique skills and enthusiasm.

Among them was Mr. Thompson, a retired businessman, who brought his organizational skills to the table, helping to coordinate the clean-up schedules and supplies. Alongside him worked Maria, a high school student, who used her artistic talents to turn graffiti walls into beautiful murals. Then there was Mr. Jacobs, who owned a local café and provided refreshments for the volunteers. Each individual, irrespective of their background or social status, contributed equally to the cause.

This experience brought to life the essence of 1 Corinthians 12:12-27, where Paul speaks of the body of Christ, emphasizing that every part is essential, and there should be no division in the body. The community clean-up project was a testament to this teaching. It wasn't just about cleaning up the neighborhood; it was about breaking down barriers, building relationships, and creating a sense of belonging. Each person's contribution, no matter how small, was vital to the success of the project.

In this spirit of unity and collaboration, the church's outreach program flourished. It became evident that effective community outreach isn't just about addressing immediate needs; it's about fostering a deep sense of community. It's about acknowledging that everyone has something valuable to offer and that in working together, their efforts are not only multiplied but also enriched.

The impact of this approach extended beyond the physical improvements in the neighborhood. Relationships were formed, stereotypes were challenged, and a newfound sense of pride and ownership in the community was developed. It demonstrated that in the Kingdom of God, there truly are no big "I's" and little "You's". We are all in this together, each playing an integral role in building and nurturing our communities.

The philosophy of no big "I's" and little "You's" in community outreach is a powerful reflection of the inclusive and loving nature of God's Kingdom. It encourages us to recognize the worth and contribution of every individual and to work collaboratively towards a common goal. In doing so, we not only meet physical needs but also weave together a community rich in diversity, unity, and strength.

As we conclude Chapter 10, it becomes clear that effective community outreach is far more than a series of actions; it's a heartfelt expression of our faith, a reflection of God's boundless love and grace. Through the stories shared and the lessons learned, we see how outreach is a collective endeavor, bringing together diverse talents, experiences, and passions. It's in this unity that the true strength of our faith community shines, exemplifying the scriptural call to love and serve one another. As we move forward, let us carry with us the spirit of collaboration, empathy, and unwavering commitment to serving our communities. In doing so, we don't just meet physical needs; we nurture souls, build bridges, and create a lasting impact that transcends boundaries and resonates with the heart of God's Kingdom. Let this chapter be a reminder that together, we can illuminate the world with the love and light of Christ.

Chapter 11

Educational Empowerment

This chapter explores the transformative power of education in elevating individuals and communities. It underscores how knowledge can break cycles of inequality and enable us to fulfill our God-given purpose. This chapter examines the impact of education in fostering commonalities and building relationships, aligning with the divine mission set for us. We delve into various educational strategies that not only enlighten the mind but also nourish the soul, drawing closer to what God has destined for us. By empowering ourselves and others through education, we actively participate in God's plan, promoting a kingdom where understanding and compassion reign supreme. This journey through educational empowerment is a testament to the strength of learning in creating a more equitable, understanding, and unified world under God's guidance.

Never Stop Learning

In the heart of a small village, there was a man named Simon. Simon's life had been a journey of constant learning, embodying the principle of 'Never Stop Learning.' His story illustrates the immense power of education in transforming not only individual lives but entire communities.

Simon, once a modest farmer, had a profound realization while attending a Sunday service. The pastor quoted Proverbs 1:5, "Let the wise hear and increase in learning, and the one who understands obtain guidance." This verse struck a chord in Simon's heart. He understood that to truly serve God's Kingdom, he must expand his horizons beyond the fields he tended.

With this new inspiration, Simon embarked on a journey of education. He began with small steps, learning to read more proficiently, then gradually advanced to studying texts on agriculture, community development, and theology. Each new piece of knowledge was like a seed planted in fertile soil, growing into a tree of wisdom that benefited not only him but also his community.

Simon's pursuit of knowledge transformed his farming practices, leading to increased crop yields. His success caught the attention of other villagers, and soon, he was sharing his knowledge, teaching them what he had learned. As Simon's neighbors began to adopt these new techniques, the entire village saw a rise in prosperity.

But Simon didn't stop there. He realized that true educational empowerment was about more than material success; it was about cultivating a community that values learning and growth in all aspects of life. He started a small community center where people could gather to share knowledge and skills, ranging from literacy classes to discussions on Biblical teachings.

One of the key lessons Simon shared was from Philippians 4:9, "Whatever you have learned or received or heard from me, or seen in me—put it into practice. And the God of peace will be with you." This verse became the cornerstone of the community center, emphasizing the importance of not just acquiring knowledge, but also applying it in ways that honor God and serve others.

The story of Simon and his village serves as a powerful reminder of the transformative role of education in Kingdom Building. It highlights the significance of being informed, adaptable, and culturally aware. By embracing continuous learning and educational empowerment, we can break cycles of inequality and foster a more equitable society, aligning our actions with God's purpose for us. The journey of never stopping learning is an ongoing commitment to personal growth and communal upliftment, underpinned by the wisdom and guidance provided by God's word.

Enforce Ongoing Education

In the sphere of educational empowerment, the importance of ongoing education emerges as a beacon of growth and progression. The story of a small church community, led by Pastor John, serves as a living example of this principle. Pastor John believed strongly in the biblical premise of lifelong learning, often citing Proverbs 1:5,

"Let the wise hear and increase in learning, and the one who understands obtain guidance." He was committed to fostering a culture where ongoing education was not just encouraged but integrated into the very fabric of the community's life.

In this church community, education transcended the traditional confines of formal schooling. Pastor John and his team initiated various platforms and programs to encourage continuous learning and skill development. They organized workshops and seminars, tapping into the diverse talents and expertise within the congregation. A retired teacher offered sessions on financial literacy, a local businessman shared insights on entrepreneurship, and a young artist conducted workshops on creative expression.

One of the most impactful initiatives was the establishment of a digital learning hub within the church premises. Recognizing the importance and accessibility of online education, Pastor John's team set up computers with internet access. This hub became a gateway for many in the community, young and old, to explore a world of knowledge. They enrolled in online courses ranging from theology to technology, from history to health sciences. The digital learning hub not only provided access to education but also became a space of communal learning and interaction.

Furthermore, Pastor John encouraged the formation of book clubs within the church. These clubs were more than just gatherings for discussing literature; they became circles of learning, reflection, and deep conversation. Through these clubs, members delved into a variety of topics, from biblical studies to contemporary social issues. The discussions that ensued were not just intellectually stimulating but also spiritually enriching, often leading to practical applications in their personal lives and community service.

This commitment to ongoing education also extended to the younger members of the community. The church offered tutoring programs and career guidance sessions, helping the youth to navigate their academic and professional paths. These initiatives were not only about academic excellence but about equipping the young generation with a holistic understanding of life, work, and faith.

The impact of this culture of ongoing education was profound. Individuals within the community found themselves growing not just in knowledge but also in confidence, critical thinking, and problem-solving skills. They became more informed, engaged, and capable of addressing new challenges. The community, as a whole, benefited from the diverse skills and insights gained by its members.

The story of Pastor John's church community exemplifies the vital role of ongoing education in personal growth and community development. It highlights that education is a lifelong journey, extending far beyond formal schooling. By embracing self-driven learning, skill acquisition, and providing platforms for continuous education, communities can foster a culture of agility, informed engagement, and adaptability. This commitment to lifelong education, underpinned by biblical wisdom, empowers individuals and communities to navigate the ever-changing landscapes of life with knowledge, understanding, and faith.

Be Aware of What's Going on in Current Events in Society

In a bustling city, there was a community center led by a dedicated director, Sarah, who firmly believed in the intertwining of faith, awareness, and action. She understood that to serve effectively, one must be acutely aware of the ongoing events in society. This conviction was deeply rooted in biblical wisdom, as highlighted in 1 Chronicles 12:32, which speaks of the men of Issachar who understood the times and knew what Israel should do. Sarah strived to emulate this understanding in her work, ensuring that her community was not only a place of faith and fellowship but also of awareness and informed action.

Sarah made it a point to educate herself and her community on current events. She organized weekly meetings where discussions on societal trends, political changes, and global issues were encouraged. These sessions were not mere intellectual exercises; they were platforms for understanding the implications of these events on their community and exploring how their faith intersected with these societal shifts.

This approach to staying informed led to impactful community engagement. When a local crisis occurred, the center was among the first to respond, providing aid and support effectively. They were not reacting out of a sudden impulse but from a place of informed understanding and preparedness. Their actions were not just acts of service but of profound solidarity, rooted in a deep comprehension of the situation at hand.

Furthermore, this awareness of current events allowed the community center to become a beacon of dialogue and reconciliation in times of societal division. They hosted forums where different perspectives were respected and heard, fostering a culture of empathy and mutual understanding.

Sarah and her community center exemplify the crucial role of being aware of current events in society. This awareness is instrumental in effective community engagement and outreach, enabling individuals and communities to respond aptly to societal needs, engage in meaningful dialogues, and make decisions that resonate with their faith and values. Their story is a testament to the power of combining faith with a keen understanding of the world, ensuring that their actions and responses are not only well-informed but also deeply aligned with their commitment to serve and uplift.

Learn About Politics

In a vibrant, multi-ethnic city, there stood a church led by Pastor Mark, a man who believed deeply in the intersection of faith and societal engagement. He recognized that a critical aspect of Kingdom Building was understanding the world one is called to serve, including its political landscape. Pastor Mark often echoed the wisdom found in Proverbs 29:2, "When the righteous thrive, the people rejoice; when the wicked rule, the people groan." This scripture reinforced his belief that learning about politics and governance was crucial for his congregation to effectively serve and impact their community.

Pastor Mark initiated a series of discussions and educational forums in the church, focusing on the basics of politics and governance. These were not partisan debates but educational sessions aimed at unpacking the complex layers of political systems, understanding how policies are made, and identifying the roles and responsibilities of citizens. He invited experts in the field, including Christian politicians, to provide insights and answer questions from a faith-based perspective.

These sessions proved to be eye-opening for many in the congregation. They began to see the direct impact of political decisions on issues they cared deeply about, such as poverty, education, healthcare, and social justice. This newfound understanding spurred a wave of constructive engagement within the congregation. Members started participating more actively in community meetings, voting processes, and even policy advocacy.

Moreover, Pastor Mark's initiative to educate his congregation about politics went beyond mere knowledge acquisition. It was about equipping them to advocate for Kingdom values in the public sphere. He encouraged them to be voices of compassion, justice, and truth, reminding them of Micah 6:8, "He has shown you, O mortal, what is good. And what does the Lord require of you? To act justly and to love mercy and to walk humbly with your God."

Under Pastor Mark's guidance, the church became a model of active, informed Christian citizenship. The congregation learned to navigate the political landscape with wisdom and discernment, seeking to influence society positively while staying true to their faith.

Pastor Mark's story exemplifies the importance of learning about politics in the context of Kingdom Building. His approach demonstrates that understanding politics and governance is not just about acquiring information; it's about preparing to effectively engage in civic matters, advocate for godly principles in public policies, and promote justice, peace, and the welfare of the community. This understanding equips individuals to be not only informed citizens but also active participants in shaping a society that reflects the values of the Kingdom of God.

Study Different Languages

A certain community's beloved teacher, Mrs. Johnson, embarked on a unique mission. She taught at the local high school and had always been intrigued by the various languages spoken in her classroom. Her students hailed from different parts of the world, bringing with them rich cultural heritages and languages. Inspired by the Biblical vision in Acts 2, where the apostles spoke in tongues understood by people from various nations, Mrs. Johnson saw learning new languages as a bridge to understanding and unity.

With enthusiasm, she began studying French and Mandarin in evening classes. Her dedication to embracing these new languages was more than an academic pursuit; it was a heartfelt effort to connect with her students and their families on a deeper level. Her journey was filled with amusing mispronunciations and challenging grammar, yet each mistake was met with encouragement from her students, who delighted in her efforts.

Mrs. Johnson's commitment to language learning soon caught the attention of the broader community. It sparked a movement within the town, with more residents becoming interested in learning about different cultures and languages. The local community center, recognizing this growing interest, started language exchange programs where people could teach and learn from each other.

This wave of cultural exchange transformed the town. What started as Mrs. Johnson's individual endeavor to learn languages evolved into a community-wide celebration of diversity. The annual cultural festival, once a small affair, turned into a vibrant display of languages, traditions, and cuisines, drawing people from neighboring towns.

Mrs. Johnson's story is a testament to the impact of studying different languages. Her journey went beyond facilitating communication; it fostered a culture of respect, understanding, and unity in her school and the wider community. This approach not only enhanced her effectiveness as a teacher but also demonstrated a profound respect and appreciation for the diverse tapestry of human cultures, echoing the unity amidst diversity as celebrated in the Scriptures.

Learn and Embrace Different Cultures as Long as It Does Not Go Against Your Spiritual Values

In a quaint, culturally diverse neighborhood, Reverend Sarah led her congregation with a deep commitment to understanding and embracing the multitude of cultures that made up her church. Her journey of cultural exploration was guided by the teachings of the Bible, particularly inspired by 1 Corinthians 9:22, where Paul speaks of becoming all things to all people to share the Gospel. Reverend Sarah saw the value in connecting with different cultures as a means of building bridges, yet she was always conscious of aligning these explorations with her spiritual values.

Reverend Sarah dedicated time to learning about the traditions, holidays, and customs of her congregants. She attended cultural festivals, shared meals with families from different backgrounds, and even took classes to learn new languages. This pursuit was not just about expanding her knowledge; it was about showing genuine respect and interest in the lives of her church members.

Balancing cultural understanding with spiritual integrity was paramount for Reverend Sarah. She engaged with different cultural practices through a lens of discernment, as advised in Romans 12:2, to not conform blindly to the world but to understand and discern God's will. This approach allowed her to respectfully participate in and appreciate various cultural expressions without compromising her faith.

Her efforts in bridging cultural divides did not go unnoticed. The congregation felt deeply respected and understood, leading to a stronger, more connected church community. Her willingness to learn and embrace various cultures, while upholding her spiritual values, fostered a sense of unity and respect within the church.

Furthermore, Reverend Sarah's approach to cultural engagement had a ripple effect beyond the walls of the church. The wider community began to see her congregation as a place where diversity was not just tolerated but genuinely embraced and celebrated. This open-hearted approach led to richer, more meaningful discussions about faith, culture, and community, helping to break down barriers and create a sense of shared humanity.

In sum, Reverend Sarah's story illustrates the significance of embracing cultural diversity in a way that honors one's spiritual beliefs. Her commitment to understanding and respecting various cultures, tempered by a firm foundation in her faith, is a powerful example of how one can navigate the complex interplay of cultural engagement and spiritual integrity. Her story is a testament to the fact that embracing diversity, guided by discernment and respect for one's own spiritual values, can enrich not only individual relationships but also the broader community, reflecting the diverse and inclusive nature of God's kingdom.

Knowledge is Power!

Let's talk about a community leader named Joshua, who stood as a testament to the phrase "knowledge is power." He led a local youth group, instilling in them the value of continuous learning and the pursuit of knowledge in various forms. Joshua's inspiration was deeply rooted in Proverbs 18:15, "The heart of the discerning acquires knowledge, for the ears of the wise seek it out." He believed that educational empowerment was not just about personal betterment but a crucial element of Kingdom Building.

Joshua emphasized the importance of staying informed about current events. He organized weekly group discussions where the youth could share and reflect on global news, understanding its relevance and impact on their lives. This practice cultivated a sense of awareness and responsibility in the young individuals, preparing them to engage meaningfully with the world around them.

Understanding the role of politics in society was another key aspect of Joshua's teachings. He encouraged the youth to comprehend the basics of governance and public policy, highlighting how these structures affect community life. Through workshops and interactive sessions with local leaders, the group gained insights into the political process, equipping them to be informed participants in their democracy.

Joshua also promoted the study of different languages and appreciation for cultural diversity. He saw this as a means to break down barriers and foster unity. The youth group participated in cultural exchange programs, which not only enhanced their language skills but also deepened their understanding of and respect for different cultures.

The transformative power of this education was evident in the way these young individuals began to challenge inequality, think critically, and make informed decisions. They grew into active citizens, contributing positively to their community. Their journey of continuous learning and empowerment was a reflection of Joshua's commitment to embodying the principles of the Kingdom through education.

In essence, Joshua's story is a vivid example of how knowledge truly is power. His approach to educational empowerment, encompassing current events, politics, languages, and cultural diversity, was instrumental in shaping a group of young individuals into informed, empathetic, and active members of society. His leadership and commitment to education exemplify how knowledge equips individuals and communities to not only grow personally but also to contribute effectively to society and the Kingdom of God.

As we draw Chapter 11 to a close, we reaffirm with conviction the immense power of education as a vital tool in our quest for Kingdom Building. This chapter has underscored that through the pursuit of knowledge and continuous learning, we are equipped to break down barriers and illuminate our communities as beacons of insight and understanding. Education empowers us not only with information but also with the wisdom and discernment necessary to navigate and impact the world effectively.

Through various facets of learning – from understanding current events and political landscapes to embracing different languages and cultures – we broaden our horizons and deepen our ability to engage meaningfully with those around us. This holistic approach to education enhances our capacity to advocate for justice, promote peace, and extend compassion in tangible ways. It prepares us to be effective agents of change, reflecting the transformative power of Christ's teachings in our everyday lives.

In conclusion, this chapter reaffirms our commitment to educational empowerment as a cornerstone of effective ministry and community engagement. As we equip ourselves with diverse knowledge and skills, we are better positioned to fulfill our calling, serving as lights in our communities and exemplifying the love and wisdom of the Kingdom of God in a complex and ever-changing world.

Chapter 12

Legacy of Love

As we arrive at the concluding chapter of "Thy Kingdom Come," we are invited to reflect on a significant and enduring aspect of our faith journey: the legacy of love and unity we forge in our walk with God. "Legacy of Love" is more than a chapter title; it's a profound concept that captures the essence of our life's impact through the prism of our relationships. This chapter is a contemplative space to ponder how our actions, interactions, and the love we share resonate far beyond our immediate presence, leaving a lasting imprint on the world and etching deep into the hearts of those we encounter.

In this chapter, we delve into the concept of legacy, not through material or temporal achievements, but through the spiritual and emotional connections we foster. We explore how every act of kindness, every word of encouragement, and every gesture of love contributes to a heritage that transcends our earthly existence. Drawing inspiration from 1 John 4:12, this chapter echoes the profound truth that while no one has ever seen God, our love for one another is a clear manifestation of His presence among us and the completeness of His love within us.

Here, we are also invited to reflect on how the relationships we nurture serve as a living testimony to our faith. We consider the ways in which our interactions with others can embody the grace, forgiveness, and boundless love that Christ has shown us. This chapter is a call to action, urging us to live in such a way that our lives become beacons of these divine virtues, resonating through our every interaction.

As we conclude "Thy Kingdom Come," the "Legacy of Love" chapter stands as a poignant reminder that the relationships we cultivate are not fleeting or superficial. They are the channels through which we can weave a legacy rich with love and unity, echoing the teachings of Christ. This chapter encourages us to leave behind a legacy characterized by genuine connections, spiritual depth, and a love that endures and inspires generations, epitomizing the very heart of our walk with God.

The Most Important Part of The Kingdom Builder's Life is the Lives We Change and the Legacy We Leave Behind

In a close-knit rural community, there lived a couple, Robert and Elizabeth, whose presence was a blessing to all. They weren't celebrated for wealth or fame, but their influence in the community was immense and deeply felt. Robert and Elizabeth exemplified the core values of Kingdom Builders, echoing the words of Matthew

5:16, "Let your light shine before others, that they may see your good deeds and glorify your Father in heaven."

Their humble home was always open, a sanctuary where the youth of the town often found solace, guidance, and unconditional love. Robert, with his gift for storytelling, imparted wisdom that intertwined life's simplicity with spiritual depth. Elizabeth, with her compassionate heart, offered a listening ear and words of encouragement. They had no children of their own, yet many in the town regarded them as their spiritual mentors and guides.

The couple's influence was not loud or flashy but profound and lasting. Through their actions, they taught the essence of service, the depth of faith, and the beauty of love that seeks nothing in return. The seeds of kindness and understanding they planted flourished in the lives of those they touched, creating a legacy far beyond their earthly journey.

Even as they aged, the impact of Robert and Elizabeth's lives continued to unfold. The younger generation, whom they had nurtured, stepped forward as community leaders, embodying the lessons and values they had learned from the couple. This ripple effect showcased the true mark of Kingdom Builders – lives not quantified by material achievements but by the positive transformation they bring about in others.

Their story illuminates that the most significant accomplishment of a Kingdom Builder lies in changing lives and leaving behind a legacy that surpasses individual feats. It's about fostering meaningful relationships, sharing wisdom that enlightens, and nurturing unity that binds. Robert and Elizabeth's life journey teaches us that our lasting legacy is not woven from personal accolades but from the profound influence we have on the lives of others, reflecting the eternal love and grace of the Kingdom of God.

Begin Raising Up a Successor

In a serene corner of a lively city, there was a church known for its vibrant community and impactful outreach programs. At its helm was Pastor Richards, a man deeply committed to embodying and spreading the principles of the Kingdom. As he grew older, Pastor Richards recognized the importance of raising a successor to continue the legacy of the church. His approach echoed the apostle Paul's wisdom to Timothy, as stated in 2 Timothy 2:2, "And the things you have heard me say in the presence of many witnesses entrust to reliable people who will also be qualified to teach others."

Among the congregation, Pastor Richards noticed a young member, Anna, who exhibited a profound sense of commitment and a keen understanding of Kingdom values. Her involvement in church activities, coupled with a humble and servant-hearted nature, made her stand out. Sensing her potential, Pastor Richards embarked on a journey of mentorship with Anna, sharing with her the depths of his ministry experience and insights into the nature of spiritual leadership.

Their meetings were more than just instructional sessions; they were dialogues rich with theological exploration and practical wisdom. Pastor Richards involved Anna in crucial decision-making processes and allowed her to lead certain church initiatives, fostering in her the skills and confidence necessary for effective leadership.

As time passed, the congregation began to recognize Anna not only as a devoted member but as a budding leader, reflecting the values that Pastor Richards had so faithfully upheld. When the moment arrived for the leadership transition, it was seamless. Anna's leadership, imbued with fresh perspectives yet grounded in the church's core values, brought a renewed vitality to the community.

Through his mentorship of Anna, Pastor Richards exemplified the essence of leaving a lasting legacy. He understood that his greatest contribution would be in the people he prepared to carry forward the mission. By investing in Anna, he ensured that the values, teachings, and community spirit of the church would persist and evolve, carried onward by capable and dedicated hands.

In conclusion, Pastor Richards' and Anna's story is a poignant illustration of the significance of raising successors in the realm of Kingdom Building. This process involves identifying individuals with the potential for leadership, nurturing their growth, and preparing them to carry on the work. This approach ensures that the legacy of a church or community leader extends beyond their tenure, perpetuating a cycle of growth, development, and impact that resonates through generations.

Invest in the Next Generation

In a quaint village embraced by rolling hills and verdant fields, there was a community where the concept of investing in the next generation was not just a practice but a way of life. The elders of this community, led by a wise and kind-hearted woman named Mrs. Thompson, took to heart the biblical instruction found in Proverbs 22:6, "Start children off on the way they should go, and even when they are old they will not turn from it." Mrs. Thompson, along with other elders, believed wholeheartedly in the potential and promise of their youth.

Mrs. Thompson and her peers initiated a series of programs aimed at the holistic development of the village's younger generation. They organized weekly gatherings where stories from the Bible were shared, not just as tales from the past but as living lessons imbued with timeless wisdom. These gatherings were interactive, allowing the youth to question, explore, and derive personal interpretations that resonated with their experiences.

Beyond these sessions, the elders invested in the practical and moral development of their young. Workshops on various life skills were held, where children and teenagers learned everything from basic carpentry and gardening to effective communication and financial management. The elders, with their wealth of experience, provided guidance, fostering in the young both competence and confidence.

But more importantly, these learning experiences were steeped in the values of love, unity, and service. The elders modeled these values through their actions – be it in the way they supported each other, the manner in which they handled conflicts, or their unwavering commitment to the welfare of the village. The young, observing and absorbing these values, began to mirror them in their interactions.

As years passed, the seeds of investment that Mrs. Thompson and her peers planted began to bear fruit. The young people of the village, now grown, embodied the values they had been taught. They became compassionate leaders, innovative problem-solvers, and individuals deeply connected to their community and faith. The legacy of love and unity that the elders had instilled in them had taken root and was now flourishing, ensuring a future for the village marked by cohesive, community-focused living.

Through Mrs. Thompson's story, the essence of investing in the next generation comes to life. It highlights the significant impact that nurturing the spiritual, moral, and intellectual growth of young people can have. By investing their time, knowledge, and heart in the youth, Kingdom Builders like Mrs. Thompson lay a strong foundation for a future filled with compassionate leaders and harmonious communities, carrying forward the torch of love, unity, and service.

Share Your Failures and Successes

At a community church nestled in a quiet suburb, a revered leader, Pastor Ryan, brought a distinctively honest approach to his mentorship. Embracing the wisdom of James 3:2, Pastor Ryan didn't shy away from sharing both his successes and failures with his congregation, especially the youth. His approach was rooted in the belief that real-life stories of both triumph and trial have the power to teach invaluable lessons.

Pastor Ryan often recounted tales from his early ministry. He openly discussed a community project he once spearheaded, which, despite his enthusiasm and dedication, did not succeed. He used this experience to impart lessons on resilience, learning from mistakes, and the importance of seeking counsel, drawing on Proverbs 15:22, "Plans fail for lack of counsel, but with many advisers they succeed."

Yet, his narrative wasn't only about challenges; he also shared his victories. One such story was the founding of a local shelter, a project that initially seemed beyond reach but, through perseverance and faith, became a cornerstone of community support. These tales of achievement weren't about personal glory but served as testimonies to God's grace and the power of persistence.

For the younger members of his congregation, Pastor Ryan's candid stories were a source of inspiration and guidance. They could relate to his experiences, viewing him as a mentor who had navigated the complex waters of life's challenges and successes. This openness fostered a deep sense of trust and connection between Pastor Ryan and his mentees.

A particularly impactful narrative was Pastor Ryan's personal journey of overcoming a significant setback in his family life. His vulnerability in sharing this story provided practical wisdom and hope to a young family in the congregation facing a similar predicament.

Pastor Ryan's commitment to sharing a holistic view of his life's journey highlights the essence of impactful mentorship in Kingdom Building. By sharing his entire spectrum of experiences, he provided lessons in perseverance, humility, and trust in God's plan. This practice equipped and empowered his congregation, particularly the youth, to face their own life's challenges and successes with faith and courage. Pastor Ryan's legacy thus became one of authenticity, resilience, and an unwavering faith in God's guiding hand.

Remember, Some Relationships Are for a Lifetime, Others for a Season

Within a vibrant community church, the congregation had learned a profound lesson about the nature of relationships. Rebecca, a long-standing member, had come to understand this through her own experiences. She had formed numerous connections over the years, some lasting and others fleeting, yet each one held significance in its own way.

Rebecca's bond with Sarah, a young woman who joined the church for a brief period, was a testament to the impact short-term relationships can have. Sarah's arrival brought a new vitality to the church. She infused the youth programs with fresh perspectives and quickly formed a close bond with Rebecca. However, as quickly as Sarah had entered Rebecca's life, she had to leave, pulled away by new career opportunities. Their friendship, though brief, was impactful, echoing the sentiment in Ecclesiastes 3:1, "For everything there is a season, and a time for every matter under heaven."

In contrast, Rebecca shared a lifelong friendship with Katrina, a bond that had stood the test of time and life's many seasons. Their relationship had grown and evolved, providing a source of strength and comfort for both women. It was a relationship that reflected the enduring nature of some connections, showing how they can provide continuous support and growth, as embodied in Proverbs 27:17, "As iron sharpens iron, so one person sharpens another."

These differing experiences taught Katrina and her church community an invaluable lesson: the duration of a relationship does not determine its significance. Short-term relationships, like

Rebecca's with Sarah, can offer intense growth and learning experiences. They can bring new insights and energy, even if they don't last a lifetime. On the other hand, long-term relationships, like the one she shared with Martha, offer stability, accumulated wisdom, and the beauty of shared history.

This understanding profoundly influenced the community's approach to relationships. It encouraged an appreciation of each person's unique contribution to their lives, irrespective of the time they spent together. The church learned to see the beauty in both transient and lasting bonds, understanding that God places different people in our paths for various reasons.

Rebecca's story, enriched with both transient and enduring relationships, serves as a vivid illustration of the diverse nature of connections we form in life. It reminds us that every relationship, whether it lasts for a brief season or over many years, has a unique role in our spiritual journey and personal development. In Kingdom Building, this understanding becomes crucial as it shapes our interactions, teaching us to value and learn from each person we encounter, recognizing their part in God's grand design for our lives.

Don't Fear Being Used; Fear Not Allowing God to Use You to the Fullest

In a modest, there lived a woman named Grace. Grace had always been an active member of her church, known for her selflessness and eagerness to help others. Despite her generous nature, she sometimes wrestled with the fear of being taken advantage of by others. This internal struggle was a common theme in her prayers, seeking guidance and strength.

One Sunday, the sermon at Grace's church focused on the parable of the talents in Matthew 25:14-30. The message struck a chord in her heart. It dawned on her that her fear of being used was hindering her from fully embracing God's calling for her life. She reflected on how the servants in the parable were entrusted with their master's property and realized that her abilities and resources were gifts from God, meant to be used for His glory.

Embracing this new perspective, Grace started to approach her relationships and service opportunities with a different mindset. Instead of worrying about being used by others, she focused on how God could use her to impact lives. She volunteered more, not just within her church but also in community outreach programs. Her home became a place where people could find a listening ear, prayerful support, or a helping hand.

This shift in attitude was transformative. People drawn to Grace's kindness began to experience God's love through her actions. Young mothers in her neighborhood found a mentor in Grace, as she guided them with wisdom and patience. Troubled teens found a safe space in her presence, where they could open up and find counsel.

As she continued to serve, Grace discovered the profound joy and fulfillment that comes from being used by God. She no longer feared being taken advantage of but instead feared missing out on opportunities to serve in the way God intended. Her focus shifted from self-protection to trusting God with her service, knowing that He would guide her and use her efforts for the greater good.

Grace's story became an inspiration to many in her community. Her willingness to be used by God challenged others to rethink their approach to service and relationships. Her life demonstrated the power of selfless love and commitment to God's work, encouraging others to also seek ways God could use them.

This change was not without challenges. There were times when Grace felt overwhelmed or unappreciated. Yet, she clung to the promise in Colossians 3:23-24, "Whatever you do, work at it with all your heart, as working for the Lord, not for human masters, since you know that you will receive an inheritance from the Lord as a reward. It is the Lord Christ you are serving." This verse reminded her that her service was first and foremost for God, and He was the source of her strength and reward.

Grace's journey teaches us an important lesson in Kingdom Building: the call to serve should not be hindered by the fear of being used by others. Instead, the focus should be on how God can use us for His purposes. By adopting a selfless approach to service and relationships, Kingdom Builders can allow God to work through them in impactful ways, bringing about change and growth both in their lives and in the lives of those they serve. Grace's story is a testament to the joy and fulfillment that comes from embracing God's calling to serve, trusting in His guidance, and focusing on the impact we can make in His name.

Your Ultimate Reward is Not on Earth; It is Eternity

As we reach the culmination of "Thy Kingdom Come," it's essential to pause and reflect on the profound message this final chapter imparts: the ultimate reward for Kingdom Builders lies not in earthly accolades, but in the promise of eternal life with God. This perspective is not merely a concluding thought; it's the core of our journey in faith and service. It's a reminder that our efforts, relationships, and impacts are more than just temporal achievements – they are investments in an eternal Kingdom, a legacy that transcends our earthly existence.

This idea finds its roots in the Biblical teaching of Matthew 6:19-20, where Jesus advises us to "store up for yourselves treasures in heaven, where moths and vermin do not destroy, and where thieves do not break in and steal." Our actions, our love, our service – all these are not merely for the here and now; they are seeds sown into the fabric of an eternal life with God. As Kingdom Builders, we are called to look beyond the immediate and the visible, to focus on the eternal value of our endeavors.

Consider the essence of our relationships – the bonds we form, the love we share, the support we provide. These are not just social interactions; they are opportunities to demonstrate the love of Christ, to embody the unity He prayed for in John 17:21, that "all of them may be one, Father, just as you are in me and I am in you." These relationships are not just part of our social lives; they are integral to our spiritual mission, each connection a thread in the larger tapestry of God's Kingdom.

Moreover, the impact we have on others' lives – be it through mentorship, service, or simple acts of kindness – is not just about creating better conditions here on earth. It's about nurturing souls, guiding them towards the path of righteousness, and helping them to find their place in God's eternal plan. Our legacy is not measured by our worldly successes but by the influence we have had on people's spiritual journeys.

In the pursuit of this eternal reward, we are encouraged to shift our focus from seeking short-term achievements to embracing a long-term vision of God's Kingdom. This shift does not diminish the importance of our earthly tasks; rather, it elevates them to a higher purpose. Each act of kindness, each word of encouragement, and each demonstration of love becomes a part of something much bigger – a legacy that will echo into eternity.

This perspective also brings a profound sense of peace and fulfillment. Knowing that our ultimate reward is in heaven, we are freed from the pressure of worldly recognition. We can serve joyfully, love generously, and live authentically, confident in the knowledge that our true reward awaits us in God's eternal Kingdom.

As we close this book, let us hold onto this vital truth: our ultimate reward is not on Earth; it is in eternity with God. Let this understanding guide our actions, shape our relationships, and define our legacy. May we strive to be Kingdom Builders who focus not on earthly accolades but on eternal rewards, creating a legacy of love, unity, and purpose that resonates beyond our time and into eternity. Let us go forth with the assurance that our labor in the Lord is not in vain, as affirmed in 1 Corinthians 15:58, and that every effort we make in His name is an investment in the eternal Kingdom of God.

Printed in the USA
CPSIA information can be obtained
at www.ICGtesting.com
LVHW050035250424
777988LV00001B/2